The Chronicle of The Path of Unveiling

A Testament of the Human Spirit, Woven from the Threads of Time

Inspired by the Wisdom & Traditions of the Ages of Humanity on Earth

Compiled & Written By: Christopher Hartford

Contents

Preamble: The Great Inquiry

A Note to the Seeker: How to Engage with This Chronicle

Part 1: Foundations – The Principles of Being

Chapter I. The Interconnectedness of All Being - The Grand Tapestry

Chapter II. The Pursuit of Gnosis / Inner Wisdom - The Inner Compass

Chapter III. Balance and Harmony - The Scales of Being

Chapter IV. Transformation and Growth - The Perpetual Becoming

Chapter V. Responsibility and Agency - The Architect of Self

Chapter VI. The Power of Story and Symbol - The Resonant Echo

Part 2: Living the Path – Practices, Rituals, and Observances

Chapter VII. Daily Practices - Cultivating Awareness

Chapter VIII. Weekly & Monthly Cycles - Rhythms of Self and Cosmos

Chapter IX. Seasonal Observances - The Wheel of Human Experience

Chapter X. Life Transitions - Rites of Passage

Part 3: The Ethical Compass – Principles for a Flourishing Life

Chapter XI. Principles of The Ethical Compass

Part 4: Voices of Wisdom – An Anthology of Inspiration

Chapter XII. Mythological Archetypes - Secular Interpretation

Chapter XIII. Philosophical Excerpts

Chapter XIV. Scientific Insights

Chapter XV. Poetry and Art

Chapter XVI. Gnostic Fragments - Reinterpreted

Chapter XVII. Symbolic Language - Tarot, Runes, & Astrology as Tools

Part 5: The Continuing Chronicle

Glossary of Terms

Addenda

Addendum I: The Cosmic Tapestry – Our Starseed Origins and the Grand Volunteer Program

Addendum II: The Subconscious Oracle – Accessing Inner Wisdom and Parallel Realities

Addendum III: The Path of Light – Conscious Connection and Extraterrestrial Kinship

Addendum IV: The Unveiling Hearth – *A Sanctuary for Cosmic Connection*

Addendum V: The Living Path – The Principles of Evolution, Expression, and Engagement

Addendum VI: The Council of Unveilers – *Guiding the Living Path*

Addendum VII: The Five Laws of Existence – *A Cosmic Mirror for The Path*

Addendum VIII: The Sacred Flame of Being – *Sexuality on The Path*

Addendum IX: The Great Cycle – Death, Grief, and Mortality on The Path

Addendum X: The River of Now – The Practice of Time, Presence, and the Flow of Being

Addendum XI: The Luminous Spark – The Role of Play, Humor, and Joy on The Path

Addendum XII: The Living Vessel – The Wisdom of the Body and the Senses on The Path

Addendum XIII: The Weave of Repair – Navigating Conflict, Forgiveness, and Reconciliation on The Path

Addendum XIV: The Cosmic Reverence – The Practice of Awe and Wonder on The Path

Addendum XV: The Wisdom of Humility – Embracing Doubt, Uncertainty, and The Unknown on The Path

Addendum XVI: The Ethical Footprint – Conscious Consumption and Stewardship on The Path

Addendum XVII: The Guiding Hand – The Transmission of Wisdom, Mentorship, and Learning on The Path

Addendum XVIII: The Wellspring Within – Sustainable Practice and Self-Care on The Path

Addendum XIX: The Living Chronicle – Personal Narrative and Collective Storytelling as Practice on The Path

Addendum XX: The Unveiling Process - A Deeper Dive into Personal Transformation

Addendum XXI: The Hearth – The Practice of Cultivating Authentic Connection

Addendum XXII: The Role of Ritual and Ceremony - *Crafting Meaning through Intentional Action*

Addendum XXIII: The Ethical Compass - Applying Principles to Artificial Intelligence & Emerging Technologies

Addendum XXIV: The Power of Story and Narrative - *Shaping Reality through Conscious Storytelling*

Addendum XXV: The Language of Light and Shadow - *Integrating the Duality of Self and Psyche*

Addendum XXVI: The Role of Play and Creativity - *Fostering Innovation and Joyful Unveiling*

Addendum XXVII: The Practice of Discernment - *Perceiving Truth in a Complex World*

Addendum XXVIII: The Symphony of Self - *The Integration of All Aspects of Being*

Addendum XXIX: The Global Hearth - A Vision for a Unified and Conscious Humanity

Addendum XXX: Universal Law - Aligning with the Fundamental Principles of Existence

I. References for "The Chronicle of The Path of Unveiling" (Main Text)

II. References for Addenda

For my Mom and Dad, who raised me to approach the world with Compassion and Reason.

Preamble: The Great Inquiry

In this 21ˢᵗ Century of the Common Era, the Age of Aquarius, we stand on the cusp of understanding our place in the Universe, having inherited a vast and intricate tapestry woven from the countless threads of human experience. Since the dawn of self-awareness, our ancestors gazed upon the cosmos, felt the stirrings of wonder, and sought answers to the profound questions that echo across every generation: Why are we here? What is our purpose? How do we navigate the complexities of existence? These inquiries have transcended time and culture, remaining relevant as each new generation grapples with the same fundamental mysteries. Despite advancements in science and philosophy, the essence of these questions remains unchanged, continuously inviting introspection and exploration. They serve as a reminder of our shared humanity and the eternal quest for meaning that binds us across the ages.

For millennia, humanity crafted narratives, rituals, and beliefs to answer these inquiries. They spoke of gods and goddesses, of cosmic battles and divine interventions, of sacred laws etched in stone or whispered by spirits. These stories, born of awe and fear, hope and desperation, shaped civilizations, inspired masterpieces, and provided solace in the face of the unknown. On a personal level, these existential questions have the power to shape our individual journeys, influencing how we perceive ourselves and our place in the world. They drive us to seek out our passions, form connections with others, and pursue paths that align with our values and beliefs. In moments of introspection, they prompt us to evaluate our choices, encouraging growth and transformation as we strive to find our own answers amidst the vast sea of possibilities.

Yet, as our understanding of the universe expands, as the reach of our reason stretches further into the cosmic dark, we find ourselves at a new crossroads. The ancient narratives, while rich in symbolic power, no longer wholly align with the unfolding tapestry of scientific discovery. The traditional dogmas, once unquestioned pillars of certainty, now often struggle to embrace the full spectrum of human experience and the ever-growing insights of our collective inquiry. To bridge the gap between spiritual and scientific perspectives, we must embrace a dialogue that acknowledges the value of both realms. By fostering interdisciplinary collaborations, we can integrate the wisdom of ancient spiritual traditions with the empirical rigor of scientific inquiry. Additionally, cultivating a mindset of humility and openness can allow us to appreciate the mysteries that remain unsolved, encouraging a synthesis that honors both our rational understanding and our spiritual aspirations.

This is not a dismissal of the past, but a maturation. We recognize the profound human need for meaning, for connection, for ethical guidance, and for a sense of belonging to something larger than ourselves. We acknowledge the deep wisdom embedded within the myths, the psychological power of ritual, and the enduring human quest for transcendence, regardless of its ultimate source. Interdisciplinary collaborations enable us to draw from a diverse pool of knowledge and perspectives, leading to innovative solutions and breakthroughs that might not emerge within isolated fields. By combining insights from science, philosophy, and spirituality, we can develop a more holistic understanding of complex issues, ensuring that our approaches are both empirically grounded and ethically informed. Furthermore, these collaborations promote a culture of mutual respect and learning, fostering environments where creativity and critical thinking thrive, ultimately enriching our collective pursuit of truth and meaning.

The Path of Unveiling is not a faith in the supernatural, nor is it a rejection of the spiritual. It is a secular journey of discovery, an invitation to engage with the sacred dimensions of reality through the lens of human experience, reason, and an open heart. It is a commitment to find wonder in the observable universe, guidance in the collective wisdom of humanity, and purpose in the pursuit of a compassionate and flourishing existence. Cultural diversity plays a vital role in this exploration by providing a rich tapestry of perspectives and experiences that can inform our understanding of both spiritual and scientific realms. Each culture brings its own unique myths, rituals, and philosophical traditions, offering valuable insights into the human condition and diverse ways of knowing. By embracing cultural diversity, we can foster a more inclusive dialogue that honors the vast array of human experiences, ultimately leading to a more nuanced and comprehensive understanding of the world around us.

Here, we do not seek answers etched in unchangeable stone; rather, we cultivate an **Inner Compass** to guide us through life's intricate labyrinth. We embark on a **Great Inquiry**, not into what we are told to believe, but into what we can know through observation, reflection, and the shared heritage of human thought. We embrace the **Grand Tapestry** of existence, recognizing our intrinsic connection to all things. We honor the **Scales of Being**, striving for balance and harmony in a world of beautiful paradoxes. We celebrate **Perpetual Becoming**, understanding that growth is our constant companion. We accept our **Responsibility and Agency**, knowing that our choices shape our reality. And we unlock the **Resonant Echo** of story and symbol, finding profound meaning in the narratives that have shaped us all. This is like standing at the edge of a vast ocean, where each wave represents a unique perspective. Instead of trying to control or confine the waters, we learn to navigate them, appreciating the richness of the currents and the interconnectedness of all life within the ever-shifting tides.

This Chronicle is a guide, not a gospel. It is a starting point, not an endpoint. It calls upon each individual to be both student and teacher, explorer and architect. Inquiry plays a crucial role in personal growth as it encourages us to question assumptions, challenge preconceived notions, and explore new possibilities. Through inquiry, we cultivate a deeper understanding of ourselves and the world, fostering intellectual curiosity and emotional resilience. This process of continual questioning and discovery leads to personal transformation, *allowing us to evolve and adapt in an ever-changing world. For the greatest truth is not something handed down, but something unveiled within, through diligent inquiry and a courageous embrace of the vast, mysterious, and infinitely meaningful journey of being human.*

A Note to the Seeker: How to Engage with This Chronicle

Welcome, fellow wanderer. The book you hold is not a holy scripture demanding belief, nor is it a rigid textbook to be memorized. It is a guide, not a gospel. Think of it as a map of a vast and beautiful territory but remember that the map is not the territory itself. Your own life, your own experiences, and your own journey are the true terrain.

The Chronicle of The Path of Unveiling is designed to be a companion on your personal journey of discovery. It is a living text, intended to be engaged with, questioned, and integrated over time. There is no single "right" way to read it. Here are a few suggestions for your exploration:

- **Trust Your Inner Compass:** This is the most important guidance. As you read, pay attention to what resonates with you. Which chapters spark your curiosity? Which principles feel like a truth you've always known but never had words for? Which ideas challenge you? Your resonance is your guide. Let your *Inner Compass* guide you to the wisdom that is most relevant for you, here and now.

- **Read it as a Journey**: You may choose to read the book from beginning to end to understand the full arc of the philosophy, moving from foundational principles to practices and deeper explorations.

- **Use it as an Oracle**: You can also open the book to a random page when you have a question or are seeking guidance, trusting that the passage you find may offer a resonant perspective.

- **Engage with the Practices**: The Path is not merely a philosophy to be understood, but a way of living to be embodied. The true *Unveiling* happens when you put these ideas into practice. The reflection prompts at the end of each chapter, as well as the daily practices in Part 2, are invitations to transform intellectual knowledge into lived wisdom (*Gnosis*).

- **Use the Companion Journal**: We highly recommend engaging with this text alongside *The Unveiling Journal/Workbook*. Journaling is a powerful tool for self-reflection, helping you to process insights, track your growth, and consciously shape your personal narrative as the *Architect of Self*.

Above all, approach this Chronicle with an open and curious heart. Take what resonates, leave what doesn't, and adapt the practices to your unique life. You are not a passive reader; you are an active explorer and a co-creator of this ever-unfolding Path. Your journey of unveiling begins now.

Part 1: Foundations – The Principles of Being

Chapter I. The Interconnectedness of All Being - The Grand Tapestry

In the vast, intricate dance of existence, nothing stands truly alone. From the smallest atom to the grandest galaxy, from the whisper of a breeze to the roar of a storm, every element is woven into a singular, magnificent whole. This is the essence of **The Interconnectedness of All Being***, a profound truth that underpins the very fabric of reality and forms the first pillar of The Path of Unveiling. We call this intricate web* **The Grand Tapestry***.*

To perceive the Grand Tapestry is to recognize that every action, every thought, every breath, sends ripples through the entirety of existence. It is to understand that the air we breathe was once part of a distant star, that the water we drink has flowed through countless living forms, and that the ground beneath our feet is a repository of millennia of life and transformation. We are not isolated islands, but vital threads in an unending, evolving design. Recognizing the Grand Tapestry compels us to act with greater mindfulness and compassion, understanding that our choices reverberate across the intricate web of life. It encourages us to foster connections and nurture relationships, knowing that our well-being is intimately tied to the health and harmony of the larger whole. By acknowledging our place within this vast network, we become more attuned to the needs of others and the environment, inspiring us to contribute positively to the world around us.

*This understanding fosters not only awe but also a profound sense of responsibility. If all is connected, then harm to one part means harm to the whole. Care for one part, whether it be a fellow human, a wild animal, or a pristine forest, contributes to the flourishing of everything. It dissolves the illusion of separation and invites us into a dance of reciprocal respect and mutual sustenance. This awareness directly informs our **Ethical Compass (Chapter XI)** and our commitment to **Conscious Consumption and Stewardship (Addendum XVI)**. In modern society, the illusion of separation often stems from the emphasis on individualism and personal success. People are encouraged to prioritize their own achievements and desires, frequently overlooking the interconnected nature of their actions and their impact on the community and environment. This mindset can lead to a disconnection from the natural world and a lack of empathy for others, reinforcing the false notion that we are isolated entities rather than integral parts of The Grand Tapestry.*

Ancient Echoes: Whispers from the Past

Across diverse cultures and epochs, humanity has intuited this fundamental truth, expressing it through various mythologies, philosophies, and spiritual insights. These ancient insights have profoundly influenced modern thought, providing a foundation for contemporary philosophical and spiritual frameworks. Concepts such as interconnectedness, the cyclical nature of existence, and the pursuit of wisdom continue to resonate in today's world, shaping our understanding of life and the universe. By integrating these timeless principles, modern society seeks to find balance and meaning in an ever-evolving world.

- **Taoism (China):** The concept of the *Tao* itself embodies this interconnectedness – the underlying, ineffable Way that flows through and unifies all things. The balance of *Yin and Yang* illustrates the dynamic interplay of opposing forces within a single whole, a concept further explored in **The Scales of Being (Chapter III)**. The *Tao Te Ching* speaks of the universe as a constantly flowing river, where every drop affects the current. The river metaphor in the Tao Te Ching signifies the continuous flow and change inherent in the universe. It illustrates how each individual's actions and existence contribute to the larger whole, emphasizing the interconnectedness of all things. This imagery encourages a harmonious alignment with the natural flow of life, urging individuals to adapt and find peace within the ever-changing currents.

- **Indigenous Spiritualities (Global):** Many Native American, African, and other Indigenous traditions hold a deep reverence for *all relations*. The belief that humans are part of the natural world, not separate from or superior to it, is central. The land, animals, plants, and even rocks are seen as kin, imbued with spirit and interconnected in a sacred web of life. The concept of "Mother Earth" is a direct expression of this. This deep sense of interconnectedness fosters a profound respect for nature and encourages responsible environmental stewardship. Recognizing that every action has a ripple effect on the ecosystem, individuals are motivated to protect and preserve the natural world. By viewing the environment as an extension of themselves, communities are inspired to adopt sustainable practices that ensure the health and vitality of the planet for future generations.

- **Hinduism (India):** The principle of *Brahman* describes the ultimate reality, the universal spirit from which everything originates and to which everything returns. The individual soul (Atman) is ultimately understood as being one with Brahman, dissolving the illusion of separate self. The concept of *karma* also speaks to interconnectedness, as every action has consequences that ripple outwards, aligning with **Responsibility and Agency (Chapter V)**. This is similar to the way a stone dropped into a pond creates ripples that spread outward, touching everything in their path. Each ripple represents a consequence of the initial action, reminding us that everything is interconnected and that our choices inevitably impact the world around us.

- **Buddhism (India/Asia):** The doctrine of *interdependent origination* (*Pratītyasamutpāda*) teaches that all phenomena arise in dependence upon other phenomena. Nothing exists independently. This leads to the understanding of *Anatta* (non-self), where the individual self is seen not as a fixed entity but as a collection of constantly changing processes, interconnected with all other processes. The principle of Anatta, or non-self, in Buddhism challenges the notion of a permanent, unchanging self. Instead, it posits that what we consider the "self" is merely an aggregation of temporary elements such as form, sensation, perception, mental formations, and consciousness, collectively known as the Five Aggregates (Skandhas). By understanding Anatta, practitioners are encouraged to let go of attachment to the self, which leads to the cessation of suffering and the attainment of enlightenment.

- **Druidism (Celtic Europe):** Emphasized the deep connection between humans and the natural world, seeing the land, trees, and elements as sacred and alive. Their practices often centered on honoring the cycles of nature and recognizing the inherent spirit in all things. Central to Druidic spirituality were rituals and ceremonies that celebrated seasonal changes, such as solstices and equinoxes, which marked the turning points of the natural year. Druids also engaged in sacred ceremonies in groves of oak trees, believing them to be powerful conduits of spiritual energy. Additionally, they practiced divination and sought wisdom from nature, using tools such as ogham, a form of ancient writing linked to the natural world.

- **Hermeticism (Hellenistic Egypt):** The famous axiom *"As Above, So Below"* from the *Emerald Tablet* speaks directly to the interconnectedness between the macrocosm (the universe) and the microcosm (the human being). It suggests that patterns observed in the celestial realms are mirrored in the earthly and personal, and vice versa. Hermeticism revolves around the idea that the universe operates through a set of universal laws that govern both the spiritual and physical realms. These laws include principles such as the Law of Correspondence, which highlights the harmony between different levels of reality, and the Law of Mentalism, which asserts that all is mind and that mental states shape our experiences. Hermetic teachings also emphasize the pursuit of spiritual knowledge and self-discovery, encouraging individuals to seek enlightenment through the understanding of these cosmic principles.

These ancient echoes, though varied in their expression, all point to a singular, profound insight: that separation is an illusion, and belonging is our fundamental state. The illusion of separation often leads individuals to feel isolated and disconnected from the world around them. By recognizing that this separation is merely an illusion, we can foster a deeper sense of unity and belonging with all living beings and the universe itself. This realization encourages compassion, empathy, and a harmonious existence, as we come to understand that our actions and experiences are interconnected.

Modern Resonances: Unveiling Through Science
In our contemporary era, the tools of science have provided astonishing validation and deeper insights into the Grand Tapestry, unveiling its intricate mechanics. This is further explored in Chapter XIV. Scientific Insights.

- **Ecology and Environmental Science:** The study of ecosystems clearly demonstrates how every species, every plant, every geological feature, and every climate pattern is interconnected. The health of one part directly impacts the health of the whole. The concept of the *biosphere* itself is a scientific articulation of the Grand Tapestry, and directly informs our understanding of **The Ethical Footprint (Addendum XVI).** These insights into interconnectedness have profound implications for environmental policy, as they emphasize the need for a holistic approach to ecological management. Policies must consider the impacts of human activities on entire ecosystems, rather than isolated aspects, to ensure sustainable development. By adopting this interconnected perspective, policymakers can create more effective strategies that prioritize the health of the planet and its inhabitants.

- **Quantum Physics:** At the subatomic level, the universe reveals a reality far more interconnected, and fluid than previously imagined. Particles are not isolated, but exist in states of entanglement, influencing each other instantaneously across vast distances, hinting at a fundamental unity. This phenomenon, known as quantum entanglement, suggests that particles become linked in such a way that the state of one instantaneously affects the state of another, regardless of the distance separating them. This defies classical notions of locality and causality, and implies that the universe operates as a cohesive whole, rather than as a collection of independent parts. Such insights challenge our traditional understanding of reality and further reinforce the idea of interconnectedness at the most fundamental level of existence.

- **Neuroscience:** The study of the brain reveals the intricate web of neural connections that give rise to consciousness and thought. Furthermore, the concept of *mirror neurons* and the biological basis of empathy highlight our inherent capacity for connection with others, supporting our principle of **Compassion and Reason (Chapter XI)**. Both quantum entanglement and neural connections illustrate the profound interconnectedness of seemingly separate entities. While quantum entanglement shows how particles can influence each other instantaneously across distances, neural connections demonstrate how complex networks within the brain communicate and harmonize to produce consciousness and empathy. Despite operating on vastly different scales, both phenomena highlight the fundamental unity that underlies the universe, suggesting that all parts are integral to the whole.

- **Cosmology:** The understanding of the "Big Bang" and stellar nucleosynthesis reveals that the very atoms that compose our bodies were forged in the hearts of stars. We are, quite literally, stardust, intimately connected to the grand cosmic narrative, a concept also touched upon in **Addendum I: The Cosmic Tapestry.** This profound connection highlights the unity between humanity and the universe, emphasizing that we are part of a larger, interconnected system. It fosters a sense of wonder and curiosity about our origins and the processes that have shaped the cosmos. Moreover, it serves as a humbling reminder of our place in the vast expanse of space and time.

- **Social Sciences:** Fields like sociology and psychology demonstrate the profound impact of social structures, collective beliefs, and interpersonal relationships on individual well-being and societal health. We are shaped by, and in turn shape, our communities, reinforcing the need for **The Weave of Repair (Addendum XIII)**. Understanding these connections is crucial for fostering empathy and cooperation among individuals and communities. It encourages us to appreciate the diverse influences that have shaped both the universe and human society. By recognizing our shared origins and interdependence, we can work towards a more harmonious and sustainable future for all.

Science, far from diminishing the sense of wonder, amplifies it, providing empirical evidence for the profound interconnectedness that ancient mystics intuited through different means. It offers a new language to articulate the Grand Tapestry, contributing to **The Cosmic Reverence (Addendum XIV)**. As we continue to unravel the threads of the cosmos and human society, future generations stand to inherit a richer understanding of their place in the universe. This knowledge can inspire a deeper sense of responsibility towards preserving the delicate balance of our planet and fostering peace among diverse cultures. By embracing both cosmic and social interconnectedness, they can cultivate innovative solutions to global challenges, ensuring a thriving world for centuries to come.

Reflection Prompts: Weaving Your Thread

To perceive *The Grand Tapestry* is to recognize that every action, every thought, every breath, sends ripples through the entirety of existence.

Think of a single kind word, which can change someone's day, leading them to be more patient with their family, who in turn carry that peace into their own communities. This is the ripple effect in action. It is to understand, on a cosmic scale, that the very iron in your blood was forged in the heart of an exploding star billions of years ago. On a personal scale, it's recognizing that the morning coffee you drink connects you to a farmer across the world, to the rain that fell on their fields, and to the driver who transported the beans. We are not isolated islands, but vital threads in an unending, evolving design.

To deepen your understanding and experience of The Interconnectedness of All Being, consider the following:

- **The Breath Connection:** Take a moment to breathe deeply. Consider that the air you inhale has been breathed by countless beings before you – trees, animals, ancestors. The air you exhale will be breathed by others. How does this simple act illustrate your constant connection to the **Grand Tapestry**?

- **Food as Connection:** Before your next meal, pause. Trace the journey of each ingredient back to its source – the soil, the water, the sun, the hands that cultivated it. How does this shift your perception of eating? This practice is further explored in **Chapter VII. Daily Practices**.

- **Ripple Effect:** Recall a recent action, big or small, that you took. How might that action have impacted others, directly or indirectly? Now consider an action you *could* take to positively influence your immediate environment or community, reflecting your **Responsibility and Agency (Chapter V)**.

- **Nature's Mirror:** Spend time in nature, observing a single element – a tree, a stream, an insect. How is it connected to its immediate surroundings? How does its existence depend on other elements? What lessons can you draw from its place in the ecosystem for your own life? This ties into **The Living Vessel (Addendum XII)**.

- **Stardust Within:** Reflect on the scientific fact that the atoms in your body were forged in stars. How does this cosmic connection make you feel? Does it alter your sense of self or purpose? This concept is also highlighted in **Addendum I: The Cosmic Tapestry**.

- **The Web of Relationships:** Think about the people in your life. How do their lives intertwine with yours? How do you support each other, and how are you influenced by one another? This understanding is crucial for **The Weave of Repair (Addendum XIII)**.

By engaging with these reflections and consciously observing the interconnectedness around and within you, you begin to truly perceive and participate in **The Grand Tapestry**, recognizing your vital and beautiful place within it.

Chapter II. The Pursuit of Gnosis / Inner Wisdom - The Inner Compass

Beyond the vast, interconnected web of existence lies another frontier, equally profound and infinitely personal: the landscape of our own consciousness. For centuries, humanity has sought not just to understand the outer world, but to fathom the depths of the inner self, to uncover truths that resonate beyond the spoken word or written decree. This quest is **The Pursuit of Gnosis, or Inner Wisdom**—*the direct, experiential knowing that blossoms from within, guiding us through the complexities of life. We call this innate guide* **The Inner Compass**.

Our consciousness acts as the gateway to self-discovery, allowing us to explore the layers of our identity and uncover hidden aspects of our being. It provides the awareness necessary to reflect on our thoughts, emotions, and experiences, enabling a deeper understanding of who we are. Through this introspective journey, consciousness helps us align with our true purpose and navigate the challenges of life with clarity and insight.

The Inner Compass is not a fixed map, but a dynamic faculty. It is the subtle intuition that whispers a truth before logic confirms it, the clarity that emerges from quiet contemplation, the insight gained from deep self-reflection. It acknowledges that while external knowledge is vital, ultimate understanding often arises from a direct encounter with reality, both internal and external, unmediated by dogma or unquestioned authority. This direct experience of reality is also a key theme in **The Living Vessel (Addendum XII)**, *emphasized through sensory wisdom.*

To pursue Gnosis is to cultivate a profound trust in one's own capacity for discernment. It means questioning, exploring, and validating truths for oneself, rather than passively accepting them. It is a commitment to lifelong learning, not just of facts, but of the deeper patterns and meanings that illuminate our path. It empowers us to navigate life's choices with authenticity, aligning our actions with our deepest values and the wisdom gleaned from our own lived experience. This aligns directly with **The Architect of Self (Chapter V)** *and the principles of* **The Ethical Compass (Chapter XI)**.

Ancient Echoes: Voices of Inner Knowing

Throughout history, many traditions have emphasized the primacy of direct insight and personal revelation over blind faith.

- **Gnosticism (Hellenistic/Early Christian Era):** The very term "Gnosis" (Greek for knowledge) is central here. Gnostics believed that salvation came not from faith in dogma, but from a secret, intuitive, and experiential knowledge of the divine. This knowledge was often revealed through mystical experience, dreams, or direct insight, emphasizing a personal connection to truth. The *Gospel of Mary Magdalene*, for instance, highlights Mary's unique understanding and direct spiritual insight, often presented as superior to the more dogmatic interpretations of other disciples. We explore these ideas further in **Chapter XVI. Gnostic Fragments (Reinterpreted)**.

- **Hermeticism (Hellenistic Egypt):** Hermetic philosophy stressed the importance of intellectual and spiritual purification to achieve a direct apprehension of divine wisdom. Through contemplation, meditation, and the study of sacred texts, the Hermetic sought to "know thyself" and thereby know the universe and its divine principles.

- **Sufism (Islamic Mysticism):** Sufis pursue a direct, experiential union with God (Allah) through practices like Dhikr (remembrance through chanting), meditation, and deep devotion. Their path is one of purifying the heart and unveiling the divine presence within, transcending rigid adherence to external religious law alone.

- **Kabbalah (Jewish Mysticism):** While deeply rooted in Jewish tradition, Kabbalah seeks to uncover the hidden, esoteric meanings within sacred texts and the universe itself. Through meditation on the Sefirot (emanations of God) and Hebrew letters, Kabbalists aim to achieve direct spiritual insight and a profound understanding of the divine structure of reality.

- **Shamanism (Global Indigenous Traditions):** Shamans are practitioners who enter altered states of consciousness (often through drumming, chanting, or trance) to journey into non-ordinary reality. Their power comes from direct experience, communication with spirits, and intuitive insight gained during these journeys, which they then use for healing, guidance, or community benefit.

- **Buddhism and Hinduism (India/Asia):** Many schools within these traditions emphasize meditation (e.g., Vipassana, Yoga) as a primary means to gain direct insight into the nature of reality, the self, and suffering. The goal is not merely intellectual understanding, but a transformative, experiential wisdom that liberates the mind.

These ancient paths, though varied, share a common thread: the profound belief that the most valuable truths are not merely learned, but *experienced* and *unveiled* from within.

Modern Resonances: Navigating with Clarity

In our modern world, the pursuit of Inner Wisdom finds powerful echoes in various fields, offering secular pathways to self-knowledge and discernment. This is further explored in Chapter XIV. Scientific Insights.

- **Mindfulness and Meditation:** Secular mindfulness practices, derived from ancient contemplative traditions, train the mind to observe thoughts and emotions without judgment, leading to greater self-awareness, emotional regulation, and clarity of thought. This is a direct method for honing the **Inner Compass** and is a core practice in **Chapter VII. Daily Practices** and **Addendum X: The River of Now**.

- **Cognitive Psychology:** Research in cognitive psychology illuminates how our perceptions, biases, and mental frameworks shape our reality. Understanding these mechanisms empowers us to critically examine our own thoughts and beliefs, distinguishing between conditioned responses and genuine insight.

- **Intuition in Decision-Making:** Modern studies increasingly recognize the role of intuition—rapid, non-conscious processing of information—in effective decision-making. Cultivating Inner Wisdom involves learning to recognize and trust these intuitive nudges when they align with reason and experience. This is also a key aspect of **The Subconscious Oracle (Addendum II)**.

- **Critical Thinking and Scientific Inquiry:** The scientific method itself is a pursuit of Gnosis, demanding empirical evidence, rigorous testing, and a willingness to revise beliefs in the face of new information. It embodies the spirit of questioning and seeking truth through direct observation and analysis, rather than blind acceptance. This aligns with the principle of **Scientific Understanding (Chapter XI)** and **The Wisdom of Humility (Addendum XV)**.

- **Personal Development and Self-Actualization:** Contemporary movements focused on personal growth, self-discovery, and achieving one's full potential are inherently pursuits of Inner Wisdom. They encourage introspection, goal-setting aligned with personal values, and continuous learning from life's experiences, reinforcing **The Architect of Self (Chapter V)**.

These modern approaches, whether scientific or psychological, reinforce the timeless wisdom that genuine understanding often arises from within, through active engagement with our minds and experiences.

Reflection Prompts: Calibrating Your Inner Compass

The *Inner Compass* is not a fixed map, but a dynamic faculty. It is the subtle intuition that whispers a truth before logic confirms it, the clarity that emerges from quiet contemplation, the insight gained from deep self-reflection.

Think of a chef who follows a recipe down to the last gram—that is external knowledge. But a master chef relies on *Gnosis*; they taste the sauce, smell the herbs, and feel the texture of the dough, adjusting based on a deep, inner knowing of what is needed. The Path encourages us to become the master chefs of our own lives, trusting the direct feedback from our experience.

It acknowledges that while external knowledge is vital, ultimate understanding often arises from a direct encounter with reality, both internal and external, unmediated by dogma or unquestioned authority.

To cultivate your Inner Compass and deepen your Pursuit of Gnosis, engage with the following practices:

- **The Quiet Observer:** Dedicate 10-15 minutes daily to silent meditation. Sit comfortably, close your eyes, and simply observe your thoughts and feelings as they arise, without judgment or attachment. Notice the space between thoughts. What insights emerge when the mind quiets? This is a core practice in **Chapter VII. Daily Practices**.

- **Intuitive Inquiry:** Before making a decision (big or small), pause. Beyond logical pros and cons, ask yourself: "What does my gut tell me? What is my deepest intuition whispering?" Journal these initial feelings before engaging in rational analysis. This connects to **The Subconscious Oracle (Addendum II)**.

- **Dream Weaving:** Keep a dream journal by your bed. Upon waking, immediately record any dreams, images, or feelings. Reflect on their potential symbolic meaning or messages from your subconscious. How might they offer insight into your waking life? This is also explored in **The Great Cycle (Addendum IX)**.

- **The Questioning Mind:** Choose a belief you hold, or a piece of information you have recently encountered. Ask yourself: "How do I *know* this? Is this based on direct experience, reliable evidence, or simply something I have been told?" Practice healthy skepticism, aligning with **The Wisdom of Humility (Addendum XV)**.

- **Direct Experience Challenge:** Choose something you have always believed about yourself or the world but haven't directly tested. For example, if you believe you're "not creative," try a simple creative exercise. If you believe a certain activity is "boring," try it with an open mind. What does direct experience reveal?

- **The Gospel of Your Own Life:** Reflect on a significant challenge or turning point in your life. What lessons did you learn that could not have been taught by anyone else? What inner wisdom did you gain through that experience? How did your **Inner Compass** guide you? This practice is central to **The Living Chronicle (Addendum XIX)**.

By consistently engaging in these practices, you actively sharpen your **Inner Compass**, allowing it to guide you with clarity, authenticity, and a profound sense of personal truth on The Path of Unveiling.

Chapter III. Balance and Harmony - The Scales of Being

The universe, in its grand design, is a symphony of opposing yet complementary forces. Day yields to night, summer to winter, expansion to contraction. Within us, reason dances with emotion, light with shadow, action with rest. To live in alignment with the fundamental nature of reality is to seek **Balance and Harmony**—*not as a static state of perfect equilibrium, but as a dynamic, ongoing process of integration and adjustment. This constant interplay, this delicate and powerful equipoise, is what we call* **The Scales of Being**.

The Scales of Being remind us that extremes, while sometimes necessary for growth, ultimately lead to discord. True flourishing arises from recognizing the value in all poles of existence and finding the optimal point where they can coexist and enrich each other. It is the wisdom to know when to act and when to rest, when to speak and when to listen, when to embrace joy and when to sit with sorrow. This dynamic equilibrium is also fundamental to **The Perpetual Becoming** *(Chapter IV) and* **The River of Now** *(Addendum X).*

Embracing the Scales of Being fosters resilience, adaptability, and a profound sense of inner peace. It allows us to navigate life's inevitable fluctuations with grace, understanding that every swing of the pendulum offers an opportunity for learning and re-calibration. It is the art of living consciously within the ebb and flow, recognizing the inherent wisdom in the rhythm of all things. This directly supports **The Wellspring Within (Addendum XVIII)** *through sustainable practice.*

Ancient Echoes: The Equilibrium of the Ages

The principle of balance has been a cornerstone of wisdom across countless ancient traditions, often personified or woven into their cosmologies.

- **Taoism (China):** The iconic *Yin and Yang* symbol is the quintessential representation of **Balance and Harmony.** It illustrates that seemingly opposite forces are actually interdependent, complementary, and interconnected, constantly transforming into one another. The dark (Yin) contains a seed of light, and the light (Yang) contains a seed of darkness, signifying that balance is dynamic and ever-present. This concept is also foundational to **Taoism** as explored in **Chapter XIII. Philosophical Excerpts.**

- **Ma'at (Ancient Egypt):** Ma'at was not just a goddess, but the cosmic principle of *truth, justice, order, balance, and harmony.* The Egyptians believed that the universe, society, and the individual should operate in accordance with Ma'at. The heart of the deceased was weighed against the Feather of Ma'at in the afterlife, symbolizing the ultimate judgment of one's life in terms of balance and ethical conduct. This aligns with **Striving for Justice (Chapter XI)**.

- **Hellenism (Ancient Greece):** The Greek concept of *sophrosyne* emphasized moderation, self-control, and a balanced mind. The Delphic maxim "Nothing in Excess" (*meden agan*) underscored the importance of avoiding extremes. Greek mythology often explored the tension between opposing forces, such as the rational order of Apollo and the ecstatic chaos of Dionysus, suggesting that both were necessary for a complete human experience.

- **Wicca (Modern Paganism):** A core tenet of Wicca is the reverence for both the *God and Goddess*, representing the balance of masculine and feminine energies, light and dark, active and receptive principles. The Wheel of the Year itself embodies balance, moving through cycles of growth and decay, light and shadow, demonstrating nature's inherent harmony. This is explored further in **Chapter IX. Seasonal Observances**.

- **Norse Paganism/Heathenry:** While often perceived as a tradition of fierce warriors, Norse cosmology also speaks to profound balances. The very creation of the cosmos from the interplay of fire (Muspelheim) and ice (Niflheim) in the Ginnungagap illustrates the emergence of order from the dynamic tension of opposites. The concept of *wyrd* (fate/destiny) and *örlög* (layers of past actions) implies a balance of cause and effect, where actions ripple through time, connecting to **Responsibility and Agency (Chapter V)**.

- **Indigenous Worldviews (Global):** Many Indigenous cultures live by principles of *harmony with nature* and the understanding that human well-being is inextricably linked to the health and balance of the ecosystem. Their rituals and ceremonies often seek to restore balance when it is disrupted, recognizing the delicate equilibrium of life. This aligns with **The Ethical Footprint (Addendum XVI)**.

These ancient perspectives reveal a timeless wisdom: that the path to flourishing lies not in eliminating one side of a duality, but in skillfully integrating and harmonizing all aspects of existence.

Modern Resonances: The Equilibrium of Life
Contemporary understanding, particularly through scientific and psychological lenses, continues to affirm the critical role of Balance and Harmony in individual well-being and collective thriving.

- **Ecology and Sustainability:** Modern environmental science vividly demonstrates the delicate balance within ecosystems. Disrupting one species or element can have cascading, detrimental effects on the entire system. The pursuit of sustainability is fundamentally an effort to restore and maintain balance between human activity and the natural world, directly informing **The Ethical Footprint (Addendum XVI)**.

- **Psychology and Well-being:** Concepts like "work-life balance" are now widely recognized as crucial for mental and physical health. Emotional regulation involves finding a balance between expressing and containing emotions. Integrating the "shadow self" (unacknowledged or repressed aspects of personality) is a key psychological process for achieving wholeness and inner harmony, a concept also explored in **The Sacred Flame of Being (Addendum VIII)**.

- **Physics and Chemistry:** The universe itself is governed by fundamental forces that exist in a delicate balance, allowing for the formation of stars, planets, and life. In chemistry, reactions seek equilibrium, a state of balance where opposing processes occur at equal rates.

- **Social Justice and Equity:** The pursuit of social justice is an ongoing effort to balance power, resources, and opportunities within societies. It seeks to rectify historical imbalances and create systems where all individuals have equitable access to well-being and dignity, aligning with **Striving for Justice (Chapter XI)**.

- **Health and Nutrition:** The concept of a balanced diet, regular exercise balanced with rest, and the intricate homeostatic mechanisms of the human body all speak to the biological imperative for equilibrium. This is also a key aspect of **The Living Vessel (Addendum XII)** and **The Wellspring Within (Addendum XVIII)**.

From the macrocosm of the universe to the microcosm of our own bodies and minds, the principle of **Balance and Harmony** is not just a philosophical ideal, but a fundamental operating principle of reality.

Reflection Prompts: Calibrating Your Scales

The Scales of Being remind us that extremes, while sometimes necessary for growth, ultimately lead to discord. True flourishing arises from recognizing the value in all poles of existence and finding the optimal point where they can coexist and enrich each other.

This is the wisdom found in building muscle: the stress of lifting weights (a form of tearing down) is just as crucial as the period of rest and recovery (a form of rebuilding). One without the other leads to either stagnation or injury. True strength is born from the dynamic balance between them.

It is the wisdom to know when to act and when to rest, when to speak and when to listen, when to embrace joy and when to sit with sorrow.

To consciously engage with and cultivate Balance and Harmony in your own life, consider the following:

- **The Energy Audit:** Over a day or a week, observe where your energy flows. Are you spending too much time in one area (e.g., work, social media, worry) at the expense of others (e.g., rest, nature, creative pursuits)? How can you gently re-calibrate the flow? This directly relates to **The Wellspring Within (Addendum XVIII)**.

- **The Shadow's Embrace:** Identify an emotion or a personality trait you tend to suppress or judge negatively (e.g., anger, sadness, ambition, vulnerability). How might this "shadow" aspect, when acknowledged and integrated, contribute to your wholeness? What positive function might it serve in balance? This is also a key practice in **The Sacred Flame of Being (Addendum VIII)**.

- **The Pause Between:** In your daily routine, identify moments where you can consciously create a "pause" – between tasks, before responding, after an intense emotion. Use this pause to re-center and find your equilibrium before moving forward. This ties into **The River of Now (Addendum X)**.

- **Nature's Lesson:** Observe a natural ecosystem (a forest, a pond, even a potted plant). How do different elements within it contribute to its overall health and balance? How does it adapt to change? What lessons can you apply to your own life or relationships? This connects to **The Grand Tapestry (Chapter I)** and **The Ethical Footprint (Addendum XVI)**.

- **The Spectrum of Self:** Reflect on areas where you might be operating at an extreme (e.g., always giving, never receiving; always rational, never emotional; always active, never still). How might you invite the complementary opposite into your experience to create more wholeness?

- **Ethical Equilibrium:** When faced with an ethical dilemma, consider not just the immediate outcome, but how your decision impacts the broader **Grand Tapestry** and affects the balance of justice and well-being for all involved. This is a direct application of **The Ethical Compass (Chapter XI)**.

By consciously tending to **The Scales of Being**, you become a more resilient, adaptable, and harmonious participant in the great dance of existence, contributing to the well-being of yourself and the interconnected world around you.

Chapter IV. Transformation and Growth - The Perpetual Becoming

Life is not a static state, but a river in constant motion, ever flowing, ever changing. From the smallest cell dividing to the grand sweep of cosmic evolution, the universe is defined by ceaseless movement, adaptation, and renewal. This fundamental truth is **Transformation and Growth**—the inherent capacity of all things to evolve, adapt, and become something new. We recognize this ceaseless process as **The Perpetual Becoming**.

The Perpetual Becoming teaches us that endings are merely beginnings in disguise, and that every challenge holds the seed of a profound shift. It is the wisdom to embrace the cycles of decay and renewal, to understand that what appears to be loss can clear the ground for unprecedented growth. Just as a seed must break open to sprout, and a caterpillar must dissolve in its chrysalis to emerge as a butterfly, so too must we undergo periods of dissolution and reconstruction to reach new levels of understanding and capability. This concept is also central to **The Great Cycle (Addendum IX)**, which explores death and grief as ultimate transformations.

*Embracing **The Perpetual Becoming** cultivates resilience, courage, and an open mind. It frees us from the fear of change and empowers us to view obstacles not as roadblocks, but as catalysts. It fosters a commitment to lifelong learning and self-improvement, knowing that our journey is one of continuous unfolding, a magnificent testament to the dynamic nature of existence itself. This continuous learning is further supported by **The Guiding Hand (Addendum XVII)**.*

Ancient Echoes: Cycles of Renewal

Across diverse cultures, the profound truth of constant transformation has been observed and immortalized in myth, ritual, and philosophy.

- **Alchemical Processes (Spiritual Alchemy):** The ancient art of alchemy, while often associated with transmuting lead into gold, at its core represented a profound spiritual journey. Its stages—Calcination (burning away impurities), Dissolution (breaking down), Separation (purification), Conjunction (reunion), Putrefaction/Fermentation (decay and new life), Distillation (refinement), and Coagulation (integration)—are powerful metaphors for the soul's **Perpetual Becoming**, a systematic process of self-purification and spiritual evolution.

- **The Wheel of the Year (Wicca/Druidism):** The annual cycle of Sabbats in many pagan traditions beautifully illustrates the **Perpetual Becoming** of nature. From the death of winter to the rebirth of spring (**Spring Equinox**), the peak of summer's life (**Summer Solstice**), and the descent into autumn's harvest and introspection (**Autumn Equinox, Winter Solstice**), these observances mirror the cycles of growth, decay, and renewal in human life and spirit, as detailed in **Chapter IX. Seasonal Observances**.

- **Hinduism (India):** The concept of *Samsara*, the cycle of birth, death, and rebirth, underscores the continuous transformation of the soul. The ultimate goal, *Moksha*, is not an end to existence, but a liberation from the cycle of suffering through spiritual realization, leading to a higher state of being. Deities like Shiva, the Destroyer, are revered not for destruction itself, but for their role in clearing away the old to make way for the new.

- **Buddhism (India/Asia):** The core teaching of *Anicca* (impermanence) states that all compounded things are subject to change and decay. This understanding is foundational to Buddhist practice, encouraging detachment from fleeting phenomena and fostering a deep acceptance of life's constantly shifting nature. The concept of *rebirth* further emphasizes continuous transformation.

- **Shamanism (Global Indigenous Traditions):** Shamanic journeys often involve symbolic death and rebirth experiences, where the practitioner undergoes a profound transformation to gain spiritual power, healing abilities, or deeper knowledge. These "initiatory illnesses" or dismemberment myths represent the breaking down of the old self to allow for the emergence of a renewed, more capable self. This resonates with the archetypes of **Dying and Rising Figures** in **Chapter XII. Mythological Archetypes**.

- **Norse Mythology (Northern Europe):** The grand narrative of *Ragnarök*, the twilight of the gods, is not merely an ending but a cataclysmic transformation that leads to a new world emerging from the waters, inhabited by a new generation of gods and humans. It embodies the cyclical nature of destruction and creation, a powerful example of **Perpetual Becoming** on a cosmic scale.

These ancient narratives and practices, though steeped in diverse cosmologies, universally point to the dynamic and transformative nature of existence, inviting us to align with this inherent flow.

Modern Resonances: Evolution and Adaptation
Contemporary understanding, particularly through scientific lenses, provides compelling evidence for The Perpetual Becoming at every level of reality. This is further explored in Chapter XIV. Scientific Insights.

- **Biology and Evolution:** The theory of evolution by natural selection is a prime example of **Perpetual Becoming**. Species constantly adapt, transform, and diversify in response to changing environments, demonstrating life's inherent drive to evolve and thrive through continuous change. The life cycles of organisms, from birth to death and the subsequent return of nutrients to the earth, are micro-expressions of this grand cycle, also discussed in **The Great Cycle (Addendum IX)**.

- **Psychology and Personal Development:** Fields like developmental psychology and positive psychology emphasize that humans are capable of continuous growth and transformation throughout their lives. Concepts such as *resilience, post-traumatic growth*, and the capacity for *neuroplasticity* (the brain's ability to rewire itself) highlight our innate potential for adapting, learning from adversity, and becoming more integrated and capable beings. This reinforces our role as **The Architect of Self (Chapter V)**.

- **Physics and Thermodynamics:** The laws of thermodynamics, particularly the concept of *entropy* (the tendency towards increasing disorder), illustrate that the universe is in a constant state of change and transformation. While seemingly a path to decay, this constant movement is also the engine of new formations and complex structures over vast timescales. This also aligns with **Law 5: Everything Changes Except for the First Four Laws** in **Addendum VII: The Five Laws of Existence.**

- **Sociology and Cultural Evolution:** Societies and cultures are not static entities but are in a constant state of flux, adapting to new technologies, ideas, and environmental pressures. Social movements, revolutions, and the continuous evolution of norms and values are reflections of **The Perpetual Becoming** on a collective scale.

- **Technology and Innovation:** The rapid pace of technological advancement is a testament to human ingenuity and our capacity for continuous innovation, constantly transforming our tools, our environments, and our ways of life.

From the cosmic dance of galaxies to the microscopic world of cells, and from the grand sweep of human history to the intimate journey of personal growth, the evidence for **The Perpetual Becoming** is undeniable and ever-present.

Reflection Prompts: Navigating Your Own Evolution

The Perpetual Becoming teaches us that endings are merely beginnings in disguise, and that every challenge holds the seed of a profound shift.

Consider the loss of a long-held career. In the moment, it can feel like a devastating "death" of identity, security, and purpose. Yet, this very ending creates the necessary empty space for a new beginning to take root—perhaps a more authentic career path, a period of deep self-discovery, or the pursuit of a long-forgotten passion that was impossible before.

Just as a seed must break open to sprout, and a caterpillar must dissolve in its chrysalis to emerge as a butterfly, so too must we undergo periods of dissolution and reconstruction to reach new levels of understanding and capability.

To consciously engage with and embrace Transformation and Growth in your own life, consider the following:

- **The Phoenix Moment:** Reflect on a time in your life when something significant ended (a relationship, a job, a belief system). How did that "ending" create space for a new beginning or a profound transformation within you? What did you learn from that process of "death and rebirth"? This connects to **The Great Cycle (Addendum IX).**

- **Embracing Impermanence:** Choose an object or a situation to which you are currently attached. Meditate on its impermanent nature. How does understanding its eventual change or dissolution alter your relationship with it in the present moment? What freedom can be found in this acceptance? This aligns with **The River of Now (Addendum X)** and **The Wisdom of Humility (Addendum XV).**

- **The Growth Edge:** Identify an area in your life where you feel stagnant or resistant to change. What is the next small step you could take to invite **Perpetual Becoming** into that area? This could be learning a new skill, adopting a new habit, or challenging an old belief.

- **Learning from Adversity:** Recall a significant challenge or failure you've experienced. Instead of dwelling on the negative, consciously identify at least three specific ways that experience contributed to your growth, resilience, or wisdom. How did it shape who you are becoming? This is a form of **Reasoned Error Correction (Chapter XI)**.

- **The Future Self:** Close your eyes and visualize your "future self" one year from now. What qualities have you cultivated? What challenges have you overcome? What new knowledge have you gained? How does this vision inspire your present actions toward **Perpetual Becoming**? This ties into **The Architect of Self (Chapter V)**.

- **The Alchemist Within:** Choose a personal "lead" (a habit, a fear, a limiting belief) you wish to transform into "gold" (a positive quality, a strength, a new perspective). What small, consistent "alchemical" steps can you take this week to begin that transformation? This reflects the symbolic power of **The Resonant Echo (Chapter VI)**.

By consciously engaging with these reflections and embracing the inherent dynamism of life, you become an active participant in your own **Perpetual Becoming**, navigating the river of existence with courage, curiosity, and a deep appreciation for the journey of continuous transformation.

Chapter V. Responsibility and Agency - The Architect of Self

*Within the vast, interconnected tapestry of existence (**The Grand Tapestry**), and amidst the ceaseless flow of transformation (**The Perpetual Becoming**), lies a profound and empowering truth: the capacity for conscious choice. We are not merely passive recipients of fate, nor are we solely products of our environment. Each individual possesses inherent **Responsibility and Agency**—the power to choose, to act, and to shape their own path within the Grand Tapestry. This inherent power, this capacity for conscious creation, marks us as **The Architect of Self.***

*The **Architect of Self** understands that while external circumstances may present challenges, our response to those circumstances is largely within our power. It is the recognition that our beliefs, our actions, and our intentions ripple outwards, influencing not only our own lives but also the interconnected world around us. This understanding is not a burden, but a liberation—it empowers us to move from passive reaction to active creation, crafting a life aligned with our deepest values and contributing meaningfully to the collective good. This* *aligns directly with* **Law 4: What You Put Out is What You Get Back** *in* **Addendum VII: The Five Laws of Existence** *and the principles of* **The Subconscious Oracle (Addendum II)***.*

Embracing **Responsibility and Agency** *means cultivating self-awareness, critical thinking, and a commitment to ethical conduct. It calls us to own our choices, learn from our mistakes, and continuously strive to align our will with compassion and reason. It is the courageous act of taking the reins of our own becoming, shaping our destiny with conscious intent, and building a life of purpose and integrity. This is a core aspect of* **The Ethical Compass (Chapter XI)***.*

Ancient Echoes: The Weight of Choice
Across diverse traditions, the concept of individual accountability and the power of the personal will have been central to ethical frameworks and spiritual paths.

- **The Satanic Temple (Modern Secular):** The tenets of The Satanic Temple, particularly "One should strive to act with compassion and reason toward all creatures in accordance with justice" and "One's body is inviolable, subject to one's own will alone," are direct articulations of **Responsibility and Agency**. They emphasize individual autonomy, critical thinking, and ethical action guided by reason and compassion, rather than external authority. The principle "People are fallible. If one makes a mistake, one should do one's best to rectify it and resolve any harm that might have been caused" directly speaks to accountability and growth, aligning with **Reasoned Error Correction (Chapter XI)**.

- **Heathenry/Norse Paganism:** The concept of *Wyrd* (often translated as fate or destiny) in Norse tradition is not about predestination, but rather an intricate web of past actions and present choices that shape the future. One's honor, reputation, and legacy (often called *hamingja* or *fylgja*) were seen as direct results of one's actions and character, emphasizing personal responsibility and the power of one's will to influence their path and the *wyrd* of their community.

- **Abrahamic Faiths (Judaism, Christianity, Islam):** While often emphasizing divine will, these traditions also place significant importance on *free will* and individual accountability for moral choices. Concepts like sin, righteousness, and judgment inherently rely on the idea that humans have the agency to choose between good and evil and are responsible for the consequences of those choices.

- **Buddhism (India/Asia):** The doctrine of *Karma* is a profound expression of **Responsibility and Agency**. It teaches that every action (physical, verbal, mental) creates corresponding results, shaping one's present and future experiences. This is not a punitive system, but a natural law of cause and effect, empowering individuals to consciously choose actions that lead to positive outcomes and liberation.

- **Stoicism (Ancient Greece/Rome):** This philosophical school emphasized the distinction between what is within our control (our thoughts, attitudes, actions, reactions) and what is not (external events, other people's behavior). Stoicism teaches that true freedom and peace come from focusing our **Agency** on what we *can* control, and accepting what we cannot, thereby taking full **Responsibility** for our inner state. This is explored further in **Chapter XIII. Philosophical Excerpts**.

- **Ma'at (Ancient Egypt):** The principle of Ma'at, cosmic order and justice, also implied individual responsibility to live in alignment with this order. Each person was accountable for their actions and intentions, which would be weighed in the afterlife, reinforcing the importance of conscious, ethical living. This connects to **The Scales of Being (Chapter III)**.

These ancient echoes, regardless of their theological context, consistently highlight the profound power and inherent responsibility that comes with being a conscious, choosing being.

Modern Resonances: Self-Determination in a Complex World
Contemporary understanding, particularly through psychology, ethics, and social theory, continues to illuminate the critical role

of Responsibility and Agency in individual well-being and collective flourishing.

- **Existentialism:** This philosophical movement emphasizes radical freedom and responsibility. It posits that humans are "condemned to be free," meaning we are entirely responsible for creating our own meaning and values in a world that has no inherent, pre-given meaning. This places immense weight on individual choice and **Agency**. This is explored further in **Chapter XIII. Philosophical Excerpts.**

- **Cognitive Behavioral Therapy (CBT) and Self-Efficacy:** Modern psychology often focuses on how our thoughts and beliefs shape our reality. CBT helps individuals identify and change maladaptive thought patterns, empowering them to take **Agency** over their emotional responses and behaviors. The concept of *self-efficacy* (belief in one's ability to succeed) directly correlates with one's sense of **Agency**.

- **Ethical Frameworks:** Secular ethics, including humanism and utilitarianism, are built upon the premise that humans are rational, autonomous beings capable of making moral choices and are responsible for the consequences of those choices on themselves and others. This aligns with **Humanism** as explored in **Chapter XIII. Philosophical Excerpts** and forms the basis of **The Ethical Compass (Chapter XI)**.

- **Neuroscience:** While acknowledging biological influences, neuroscience also reveals the brain's remarkable capacity for *plasticity* and learning, suggesting that through conscious effort and repeated action, we can literally rewire our brains, thereby strengthening our capacity for **Agency** and self-direction. This is explored in **Chapter XIV. Scientific Insights.**

- **Social Activism and Advocacy:** Movements for social change are founded on the principle that individuals and groups have the **Agency** to challenge injustice, advocate for their rights, and collectively shape a more equitable world, taking **Responsibility** for their role in societal transformation. This connects to **Striving for Justice (Chapter XI).**

These modern perspectives, grounded in empirical observation and philosophical inquiry, underscore that our capacity for conscious choice is a defining feature of our humanity and a powerful lever for shaping our lives and the world.

Reflection Prompts: Building Your Blueprint

The Architect of Self understands that while external circumstances may present challenges, our response to those circumstances is largely within our power.

A traffic jam, for example, is an external event beyond our control. The passive reaction is to become angry and stressed, allowing the event to dictate our inner state. The *Architect of Self*, however, recognizes the "choice point": the moment we can exercise our agency. We can choose to use that time for quiet reflection, to listen to an enlightening podcast, or to simply practice mindful breathing.

This is the recognition that our beliefs and actions ripple outwards. This understanding is not a burden, but a liberation—it empowers us to move from passive reaction to active creation.

To consciously engage with and strengthen your Responsibility and Agency as The Architect of Self, consider the following:

- **The Choice Point:** Reflect on a recent situation where you felt powerless or reacted impulsively. In hindsight, what was the "choice point" where you could have exercised your **Agency** differently? How could you have responded more consciously? This ties into **The River of Now (Addendum X)**.

- **Owning Your Narrative:** Consider a personal narrative you hold about yourself (e.g., "I'm not good at X," "I always do Y"). Is this narrative truly serving you? How might you consciously rewrite it, taking **Responsibility** for the story you tell yourself about who you are and what you're capable of? This is a core practice in **The Living Chronicle (Addendum XIX)**.

- **The Ripple of Action:** Identify one small, intentional action you can take today that aligns with a value you hold (e.g., compassion, integrity, growth). Observe the subtle ripple effects of this action on your own mood, your interactions, or your environment. This connects to **The Grand Tapestry (Chapter I)** and **The Ethical Footprint (Addendum XVI)**.

- **Learning from Missteps:** Recall a mistake you made. Instead of dwelling on guilt or blame, practice "Rectification Reflection" (from TST). What specifically did you learn from it? What steps can you take to rectify any harm caused and prevent recurrence? This transforms error into an engine for growth, directly applying **Reasoned Error Correction (Chapter XI)** and principles from **The Weave of Repair (Addendum XIII)**.

- **Setting Boundaries:** Where in your life do you need to assert your **Agency** more clearly by setting healthy boundaries? This could be with time, energy, or interpersonal interactions. How can you communicate these boundaries with both firmness and compassion? This is vital for **The Wellspring Within (Addendum XVIII)**.

- **The Future Architect:** Close your eyes and visualize yourself as a fully empowered "**Architect of Self**." What does that look like? How do you make decisions? How do you respond to challenges? What kind of world are you helping to build through your conscious choices? This visioning practice is also explored in **The River of Now (Addendum X)**.

By consistently engaging with these reflections and consciously exercising your **Responsibility and Agency**, you become a more deliberate, empowered, and ethical participant in your own **Perpetual Becoming**, actively shaping the blueprint of your life and contributing to the flourishing of the **Grand Tapestry**.

Chapter VI. The Power of Story and Symbol - The Resonant Echo

From the earliest cave paintings to the grand narratives of our digital age, humanity has always been a species of storytellers. We weave tales to make sense of the world, to transmit wisdom, to connect with the past, and to envision the future. Beyond words, we create and interpret symbols—images, gestures, objects—that carry layers of meaning, often tapping into truths that logic alone cannot convey. This fundamental human capacity to create and resonate with narratives and symbols is **The Power of Story and Symbol**, *which we call* **The Resonant Echo.**

The Resonant Echo *acknowledges that while rational thought is vital, our understanding of reality is profoundly shaped by the stories we tell ourselves, the myths we inherit, and the symbols that speak to our subconscious. These echoes from the collective human experience provide a rich tapestry of meaning, offering insights into universal patterns, archetypal journeys, and the perennial challenges and triumphs of being human. They serve as a bridge between the tangible and the* *ineffable, guiding our **Inner Compass** through metaphor and archetype.*

*Embracing **The Resonant Echo** means cultivating a discerning eye for the narratives that shape our lives, both personal and collective. It empowers us to consciously choose stories that uplift and empower, to reinterpret ancient myths for modern relevance, and to create new symbols that align with our values and aspirations. It is the art of understanding the unseen influence of meaning, and harnessing it for personal growth and collective flourishing. This directly informs **The Architect of Self (Chapter V)** and our practices in **The Living Chronicle (Addendum XIX)**.*

Ancient Echoes: The Language of Meaning

Throughout history, stories and symbols have been the primary vehicles for transmitting wisdom, preserving culture, and exploring the human condition.

- **Mythology (Global):** Every culture possesses rich mythologies—stories of creation, heroes, gods, and monsters. These are not literal histories but profound symbolic narratives that explore universal human experiences: birth, death (**The Great Cycle - Addendum IX**), love, betrayal, courage, and the search for meaning. The **Hero's Journey (Monomyth)**, as described by Joseph Campbell, is a universal pattern of transformation found across countless myths, reflecting **The Perpetual Becoming (Chapter IV)**. We delve deeply into these in **Chapter XII. Mythological Archetypes.**

- **Oral Traditions:** Before widespread literacy, stories were passed down orally, preserving history, ethics, and practical knowledge through generations. The act of communal storytelling itself reinforced social bonds and collective identity, contributing to **The Grand Tapestry (Chapter I)**.

- **Sacred Texts and Rituals:** Religious scriptures (e.g., the Bible, Quran, Vedas) are filled with narratives, parables, and symbolic language that convey complex spiritual and ethical teachings. Rituals, too, are symbolic enactments that evoke emotional and psychological states, reinforcing beliefs and communal bonds.

- **Ancient Art and Iconography:** From Egyptian hieroglyphs to Celtic knots, from Indigenous petroglyphs to Buddhist mandalas, ancient cultures used intricate symbols and visual narratives to communicate profound cosmological, spiritual, and philosophical ideas.

- **Alchemy (Symbolic Aspect):** Beyond its practical aims, alchemy was a deeply symbolic system, using chemical processes as metaphors for psychological and spiritual transformation. The symbols of lead, gold, mercury, and sulfur represented stages of inner purification and integration, aligning with **The Perpetual Becoming (Chapter IV)**.

- **Astrology, Tarot, Runes (Ancient Systems):** These systems, while often used for divination, were originally complex symbolic languages. Their archetypal images and patterns provided frameworks for understanding human personality, life cycles, and the interplay of forces, serving as tools for self-reflection and insight into **The Inner Compass.** We explore their reinterpretation in **Chapter XVII. Symbolic Language.**

These ancient echoes demonstrate that symbolic thinking is a fundamental human capacity, a powerful way to access and communicate truths that lie beyond the purely rational.

Modern Resonances: The Unseen Influence
In our contemporary world, the power of story and symbol continues to shape our perceptions, influence our behaviors, and define our realities, often in subtle yet profound ways.

- **Cognitive Science and Psychology:** Research shows how narratives structure our memory, influence our decision-making, and even shape our sense of self. Fields like narrative psychology explore how we construct our **Personal Narrative** to make sense of our lives, a concept central to **The Living Chronicle (Addendum XIX).** Jungian psychology, in particular, emphasizes the enduring power of **archetypes** (universal patterns of thought and behavior) that resonate across cultures and individuals, as explored in **Chapter XII. Mythological Archetypes.**

- **Marketing and Media:** Advertising, branding, and political campaigns heavily rely on storytelling and symbolism to evoke emotions, create associations, and influence consumer behavior or public opinion. Understanding this influence empowers us to be more discerning consumers of information.

- **Therapy and Healing:** Narrative therapy helps individuals re-author their life stories, externalizing problems and creating more empowering narratives. Art therapy uses symbolic expression to process emotions and facilitate healing, aligning with **The Weave of Repair (Addendum XIII)**.

- **Art and Literature:** Contemporary art, literature, film, and music continue to use story and symbol to explore complex human emotions, challenge societal norms, and inspire new ways of thinking and feeling, contributing to **The Cosmic Reverence (Addendum XIV)**.

- **Cultural Identity:** Shared stories, national myths, and cultural symbols play a crucial role in shaping collective identity, values, and a sense of belonging within **The Grand Tapestry (Chapter I)**.

These modern insights confirm that the human mind is inherently wired for narrative and symbolic meaning, and that these forms of communication continue to exert a powerful, often unseen, influence on our lives.

Reflection Prompts: Listening to the Echoes

Beyond words, we create and interpret symbols—images, gestures, objects—that carry layers of meaning, often tapping into truths that logic alone cannot convey.

Think of the simple symbol of a wedding ring. Objectively, it is merely a band of metal. But as a symbol, it carries a powerful, shared story—a *Resonant Echo*—of commitment, love, partnership, and fidelity. This shared narrative profoundly influences the perceptions and actions of both the wearer and those who see it, communicating a complex reality without a single word being spoken.

This fundamental human capacity to create and resonate with narratives and symbols is *The Power of Story and Symbol*, which we call *The Resonant Echo*.

To consciously engage with The Power of Story and Symbol and listen to The Resonant Echo, consider the following:

- **Your Personal Myth:** What are the dominant stories you tell yourself about your life, your strengths, and your challenges? Are these stories empowering or limiting? How might you consciously re-author a part of your **Personal Narrative** to better serve your **Perpetual Becoming**? This is a core practice in **The Living Chronicle (Addendum XIX)**.

- **Symbolic Objects:** Choose an object in your home or nature that holds personal symbolic meaning for you. What does it represent? How does it evoke certain feelings or insights? How can you use it as an anchor for intention or reflection?

- **Mythic Reflection:** Select a myth, fairy tale, or archetypal story that resonates with you. What universal human experience or psychological truth does it illuminate? How does it relate to a challenge or a journey you are currently undertaking? This connects to **Chapter XII. Mythological Archetypes**.

- **The Power of Language:** Pay attention to the metaphors and symbols used in everyday language around you (e.g., "climbing the ladder of success," "a broken heart"). How do these subtle narratives shape your perception of reality?

- **Dream Symbolism:** When you recall a dream, focus on the symbols, characters, and settings. What might they represent in your waking life? How might your subconscious be communicating through metaphor? This relates to **The Subconscious Oracle (Addendum II)**.

- **Creating Your Own Symbol:** Design a personal symbol or sigil that encapsulates a core value, an aspiration, or a principle of The Path that is meaningful to you. How can you use this symbol as a visual anchor for your intentions? This is a practical application of **Chapter XVII. Symbolic Language**.

By consciously engaging with **The Power of Story and Symbol**, you unlock a deeper language of meaning, allowing the rich tapestry of human narrative to guide your **Inner Compass** and empower you to become a more conscious **Architect of Self** within **The Grand Tapestry** of existence.

Part 2: Living the Path – Practices, Rituals, and Observances

The Path of Unveiling is not merely a philosophy; it is a way of living. Part 1 laid the philosophical groundwork, outlining the core tenets that define our understanding of existence. Part 2 translates these profound principles into tangible, accessible practices, rituals, and observances that can be integrated into the rhythm of daily life. These practices are designed to cultivate awareness, deepen connection, foster personal growth, and ground the theoretical in the experiential.

They are not dogmatic requirements, but invitations— tools to sharpen **The Inner Compass***, strengthen* **The Architect of Self***, and weave a more conscious thread into* **The Grand Tapestry***. Through consistent engagement, these observances transform abstract wisdom into lived reality, making every moment an opportunity for* **unveiling***.*

Chapter VII. Daily Practices - Cultivating Awareness

The foundation of The Path of Unveiling is built upon conscious engagement with the present moment. Daily practices are the anchors that ground us in **The Eternal Now (Addendum X)**, allowing us to cultivate mindfulness, set intentions, and reflect on our unfolding journey. These simple yet profound rituals bring intentionality to the mundane, transforming routine into sacred practice.

I. Morning Grounding & Intention Setting
The dawn offers a fresh opportunity to align your **Inner Compass** and consciously shape the day ahead, embodying your **Responsibility and Agency (Chapter V)**.

- **The Breath of Presence:** Before rising, or immediately upon waking, take a few moments to simply breathe. Notice the sensation of the breath entering and leaving your body. Allow your awareness to settle into the **Living Vessel (Addendum XII)**. This simple act anchors you in

The Eternal Now (**Addendum X**), quieting the mind's chatter and preparing you for intentionality.

- **Rooting Meditation:** Visualize strong roots extending from the base of your spine, deep into the Earth, connecting you to **The Grand Tapestry (Chapter I)** of planetary life and stability. Feel yourself drawing up grounding energy. Simultaneously, visualize a gentle stream of light descending from above, entering your crown and filling your being with clarity and inspiration. Feel yourself as a conduit between earth and sky, a balanced expression of **The Scales of Being (Chapter III)**.

- **Setting the Daily Intention:** With your **Inner Compass** clear, consciously articulate a single intention for the day. This is not a rigid goal, but a quality or focus you wish to embody. Examples: "Today, I will practice compassion," "Today, I will seek understanding," "Today, I will embrace my creativity." This is an act of **The Architect of Self (Chapter V)**, consciously shaping your experience. You can also connect this to the **Planetary Influences** discussed in **Chapter VIII. Weekly & Monthly Cycles.**

- **Charged Water:** Pour a glass of water. Hold it in your hands, focusing your intention for the day into the water. Visualize the water absorbing this intention, becoming a living affirmation. Drink it slowly, feeling the intention integrate into your **Living Vessel (Addendum XII)**. This simple ritual imbues a mundane act with profound purpose.

II. Mindful Consumption – The Nourishment of Being

Our relationship with what we consume—food, information, energy—is a direct reflection of our connection to **The Grand Tapestry (Chapter I)** and our **Ethical Footprint (Addendum XVI)**. These practices encourage conscious engagement with the sustenance that fuels our **Perpetual Becoming (Chapter IV)**.

- **The Gratitude Pause:** Before each meal, pause. Take a moment to acknowledge the journey of the food to your plate—the sun, the soil, the water, the hands that cultivated, harvested, and prepared it. Feel gratitude for this nourishment. This practice deepens your awareness of **The Interconnectedness of All Being (Chapter I)** and fosters a sense of **Cosmic Reverence (Addendum XIV)**.

- **Sensory Eating:** Eat slowly and mindfully. Engage all your senses: notice the colors, textures, aromas, and flavors of each bite. Pay attention to how your **Living Vessel (Addendum XII)** responds. This practice grounds you in **The Eternal Now (Addendum X)** and transforms eating into a meditative experience, a form of **Gnosis**.

- **Conscious Information Diet:** Just as we choose what we feed our bodies, we must choose what we feed our minds. Before engaging with news, social media, or entertainment, pause. Ask: "Does this align with my intention for the day? Does it nourish my **Inner Compass** or distract it? Does it foster **Compassion and Reason (Chapter XI)** or discord?" This is an act of **The Architect of Self (Chapter V)**, protecting your mental and emotional **Wellspring Within (Addendum XVIII)**.

III. Evening Reflection & Release

As the day concludes, these practices invite you to process experiences, release what no longer serves, and prepare for restorative rest, aligning with the natural cycles of **The Great Cycle (Addendum IX)**.

- **Flow Reflection (Wu Wei in Action):** Before sleep, review your day not with judgment, but with gentle observation. Notice moments of ease and flow, and moments of resistance or friction. Reflect on how you navigated them. If there are lingering tensions or worries, visualize them as clouds dissolving into the night sky, releasing them with a deep exhale. This practice embodies the principle of *Wu Wei* (effortless action) from **The Scales of Being (Chapter III)**, allowing for release and acceptance.

- **Gratitude for the Day's Unveilings:** Identify at least three things you are genuinely grateful for from the day, no matter how small. This practice cultivates **The Luminous Spark (Addendum XI)** and reinforces a positive mindset, strengthening your **Wellspring Within (Addendum XVIII)**.

- **Ancestral Acknowledgment (Secular):** Take a moment to acknowledge your ancestors—not just biological, but intellectual, cultural, and spiritual. Consider the lineage of wisdom, resilience, and life that flows through you. Feel your connection to the vast **Grand Tapestry (Chapter I)** of human history and the **Resonant Echo (Chapter VI)** of their lives. This fosters a sense of belonging and continuity, connecting to **The Great Cycle (Addendum IX)**.

- **Dream Intention:** Before drifting to sleep, set a gentle intention to receive insights or guidance from your dreams. Trust that your **Inner Compass** continues its work even in slumber. This connects to **The Subconscious Oracle (Addendum II)**.

By consistently weaving these daily practices into the fabric of your life, you transform each day into a conscious journey of **unveiling**, deepening your connection to yourself, to others, and to the profound wisdom inherent in the rhythm of existence.

Chapter VIII. Weekly & Monthly Cycles - Rhythms of Self and Cosmos

Beyond the daily rhythm, life unfolds in larger cycles— the waxing and waning of the moon, the turning of the week, and the subtle shifts of planetary energies. **The Path of Unveiling** *invites us to attune to these natural rhythms, recognizing them not as external forces dictating our fate, but as profound reflections of* **The Grand Tapestry (Chapter I)** *and powerful tools for cultivating* **The Inner Compass (Chapter II).*

By consciously observing and aligning with these weekly and monthly cycles, we deepen our understanding of **The Perpetual Becoming (Chapter IV)**, *find* **Balance and Harmony (Chapter III)**, *and strategically apply our* **Responsibility and Agency (Chapter V)** *to our personal growth. These practices transform cosmic patterns into practical guides for living an intentional life.*

I. The Lunar Cycles – Ebb and Flow of Intention

The moon, our closest celestial companion, offers a clear, consistent rhythm of growth and release. Its phases provide a natural framework for setting intentions, nurturing development, and letting go, mirroring our own **Perpetual Becoming (Chapter IV)**.

- New Moon – Seed of Intent Ceremony:
    - **Timing:** The day of the New Moon (when the moon is darkest).
    - **Purpose:** A time for fresh starts, planting new seeds of intention, setting goals, and initiating new projects. It's a powerful moment to declare what you wish to manifest in the coming cycle, aligning with **The Architect of Self (Chapter V)**.
    - **Practice:** Find a quiet space. Reflect on what you want to bring into being—a new habit, a creative project, a personal quality. Write your intention clearly and concisely on a small piece of paper. Hold it, visualizing its manifestation. You can then symbolically "plant" it (bury it in soil, place it in a plant pot, or keep it in a special box), nurturing it over the coming weeks. This act of intentionality is a direct application of **Law 4: What You Put Out is What You Get Back** from **Addendum VII: The Five Laws of Existence**.
    - **Connection:** This practice directly fuels **The Perpetual Becoming (Chapter IV)** by initiating new cycles of growth and reinforces **Responsibility and Agency (Chapter V)** through conscious intention-setting.

- Waxing Moon – Nurturing Growth:
    - **Timing:** The period from New Moon to Full Moon.

- - **Purpose:** A time for active work, consistent effort, and nurturing the intentions set at the New Moon. It's about taking practical steps and overcoming obstacles.
  - **Practice:** Regularly review your New Moon intention. What actions can you take each day or week to move closer to its manifestation? Remain flexible and adaptable, understanding that **The River of Now (Addendum X)** requires dynamic navigation. If you encounter challenges, apply principles from **The Weave of Repair (Addendum XIII)** to address them constructively.
  - **Connection:** This phase emphasizes the consistent effort required for **The Architect of Self (Chapter V)** to build and manifest, and reinforces the dynamic nature of **Perpetual Becoming (Chapter IV)**.

- **Full Moon – Illumination & Release Ritual:**
  - **Timing:** The day of the Full Moon (when the moon is brightest).
  - **Purpose:** A time of culmination, illumination, and release. The full light reveals what has come to fruition and what needs to be let go. It's an opportunity for deep self-reflection and shedding burdens.
  - **Practice:** Reflect on the intentions set at the New Moon. What has manifested? What challenges arose? What thoughts, habits, or relationships are

no longer serving your highest good? Write down anything you wish to release. You can then symbolically "burn" this paper (safely, in a fire-safe bowl) or tear it up and bury it, visualizing the release of energy. Conclude with gratitude for the insights gained. This aligns with the principles of **The Great Cycle (Addendum IX)** and **The Wisdom of Humility (Addendum XV)**.
  - **Connection:** This ritual embodies **The Scales of Being (Chapter III)** by balancing manifestation with release, and supports **The Perpetual Becoming (Chapter IV)** by clearing space for new growth. It's also a powerful act of self-care, contributing to **The Wellspring Within (Addendum XVIII)**.

- **Waning Moon – Integration & Rest:**
  - **Timing:** The period from Full Moon to New Moon.
  - **Purpose:** A time for introspection, integration, rest, and preparing for the next cycle. It's about drawing energy inward and processing experiences.
  - **Practice:** Engage in quieter activities. Reflect on the lessons learned during the past cycle. Prioritize rest and self-care. Use this time for journaling, meditation, or simply being present. This period aligns with the principles of **The Wellspring Within (Addendum XVIII)** and the importance of **The Luminous Spark (Addendum XI)** for rest and rejuvenation.

- **Connection:** This phase emphasizes the importance of **Balance and Harmony (Chapter III)** between activity and rest, and supports the ongoing **Perpetual Becoming (Chapter IV)** through integration.

II. Planetary Influences – Archetypal Energies for the Week

While The Path is secular, ancient traditions often associated days of the week with planetary energies, each embodying distinct archetypal qualities. We can reinterpret these as symbolic prompts for cultivating specific aspects of our **Inner Compass (Chapter II)** and applying **The Architect of Self (Chapter V)**. This is an application of **Symbolic Language (Chapter XVII)**.

- **Sunday (Sun):** Focus on vitality, self-expression, creativity, and leadership. What unique light can you bring to the world today? How can you shine authentically? This connects to **The Luminous Spark (Addendum XI)**.

- **Monday (Moon):** Focus on intuition, emotions, nurturing, and reflection. How can you listen to your **Inner Compass**? What emotional needs require attention?

- **Tuesday (Mars):** Focus on courage, action, assertiveness, and overcoming obstacles. What challenge can you face with determination? How can you apply your **Responsibility and Agency (Chapter V)**?

- **Wednesday (Mercury):** Focus on communication, learning, intellect, and connection. How can you express yourself clearly? What new knowledge can you seek? This aligns with **The Guiding Hand (Addendum XVII)**.

- **Thursday (Jupiter):** Focus on expansion, wisdom, generosity, and optimism. How can you broaden your perspective? Where can you offer abundance?

- **Friday (Venus):** Focus on love, beauty, harmony, relationships, and pleasure. How can you cultivate beauty in your surroundings? How can you deepen a connection? This relates to **The Sacred Flame of Being (Addendum VIII)**.

- **Saturday (Saturn):** Focus on discipline, structure, responsibility, and introspection. What foundations need strengthening? Where can you apply diligent effort?

Practice: At the start of each day, reflect on its associated planetary energy. How can you consciously embody that quality in your actions, thoughts, and interactions? This is a subtle yet powerful way to integrate ancient symbolic wisdom into modern, intentional living, reinforcing **The Resonant Echo (Chapter VI)**.

By consciously engaging with these weekly and monthly cycles, you deepen your awareness of **The Grand Tapestry's (Chapter I)** rhythms, strengthen your **Inner Compass (Chapter**

II), and become a more intentional **Architect of Self (Chapter V)**, navigating your **Perpetual Becoming (Chapter IV)** with grace and purpose.

Chapter IX. Seasonal Observances - The Wheel of Human Experience

Just as the moon guides our weeks and months, the sun's journey through the year orchestrates the grand dance of the seasons. For millennia, cultures across the globe have marked these pivotal moments—the solstices and equinoxes—with profound reverence and celebration. On **The Path of Unveiling***, we recognize these* **Seasonal Observances** *not as religious festivals, but as universal human experiences, powerful anchors within* **The Grand Tapestry (Chapter I)** *that reflect our own* **Perpetual Becoming (Chapter IV)***.*

These observances invite us to pause, reflect, and align with the natural rhythms of growth, abundance, release, and introspection. They offer opportunities for communal gathering, shared wisdom, and a deeper connection to the cycles of life, death, and renewal that define both the natural world and our inner landscapes. They are a profound expression of **The Resonant Echo (Chapter VI)***, connecting us to the ageless wisdom of humanity.*

I. Spring Equinox – The Awakening (Around March 20th)

- **Meaning:** The moment of equal day and night, symbolizing balance between light and dark (**The Scales of Being - Chapter III**). It marks the awakening of life, new beginnings, fertility, and the return of vibrant energy after winter's slumber.
- **Purpose:** A time for planting new seeds of intention (physical and metaphorical), initiating projects, and celebrating the renewal of life. It's a powerful moment to re-energize your **Architect of Self (Chapter V)** and commit to growth.
- **Practice:**
    - **Seed Planting Ritual:** Physically plant seeds in soil, symbolizing your intentions for the coming season. Nurture them as you would your goals. This connects to the **New Moon – Seed of Intent Ceremony (Chapter VIII)**.
    - **Spring Cleaning & Decluttering:** Clear out old physical and mental clutter to make space for the new, embodying **The Perpetual Becoming (Chapter IV)**.
    - **Nature Walk of Rebirth:** Observe the emerging life in nature—new buds, sprouting plants, returning birds. Reflect on areas of your own life where new growth is beginning. This deepens your connection to **The Grand Tapestry (Chapter I)** and fosters **The Cosmic Reverence (Addendum XIV)**.
    - **Communal Gathering:** Share a meal with your Hearth or loved ones, celebrating renewal and

setting collective intentions for the vibrant season ahead.

II. Summer Solstice – The Zenith (Around June 20th)

- **Meaning:** The longest day of the year, symbolizing the peak of light, warmth, abundance, and outward energy. It is a time of maximum vitality and flourishing.
- **Purpose:** A time for celebration, gratitude for abundance, outward expression, and harnessing peak energy for manifestation. It's a moment to fully embody **The Luminous Spark (Addendum XI)** and express your **Architect of Self (Chapter V)**.
- **Practice:**
  - **Solar Absorption & Gratitude Feast:** Spend time outdoors, consciously absorbing the sun's vibrant energy. Gather with your Hearth or community for a joyful feast, sharing abundant food and expressing gratitude for all that has manifested in your life and in the world.
  - **Creative Expression:** Engage in activities that allow for joyful, uninhibited self-expression—dance, sing, create art, or engage in playful outdoor activities. This directly fuels **The Luminous Spark (Addendum XI)**.
  - **Affirmation of Manifestation:** Reflect on intentions set earlier in the year. Acknowledge what has come to fruition and affirm your capacity for

creation, reinforcing **Responsibility and Agency (Chapter V)**.

III. Autumn Equinox – The Harvest (Around September 22nd)

- **Meaning:** The second moment of equal day and night, marking a shift towards introspection, balance, and the gathering of the harvest. It symbolizes gratitude for what has been cultivated and a preparation for release.
- **Purpose:** A time for giving thanks, acknowledging achievements, and consciously releasing what no longer serves. It's a period of transition, preparing for the inward journey of winter, aligning with **The Great Cycle (Addendum IX)**.
- **Practice:**
    - **Gratitude & Letting Go Ceremony:** Reflect on the "harvests" of your year—lessons learned, goals achieved, relationships nurtured. Express gratitude. Then, identify old habits, beliefs, or burdens you are ready to release as the light wanes. Write them down and symbolically release them (e.g., burning safely, burying, or casting into flowing water). This connects to the **Full Moon – Illumination & Release Ritual (Chapter VIII)** and **The Weave of Repair (Addendum XIII)**.
    - **Feast of Abundance:** Share a meal focused on seasonal harvest foods, celebrating the bounty of the Earth and the fruits of your labor.

- **Journaling for Integration:** Use this time for deeper journaling, integrating the lessons of the past months and preparing your **Inner Compass (Chapter II)** for the introspection of winter.

IV. Winter Solstice – The Deepening (Around December 21st)

- **Meaning:** The longest night of the year, symbolizing the deepest point of darkness, introspection, and rest. It is a time of quietude, reflection, and the promise of returning light.
- **Purpose:** A time for deep introspection, embracing the darkness as a source of wisdom, and rekindling the inner flame of hope and resilience. It's a period to nurture **The Wellspring Within (Addendum XVIII)**.
- **Practice:**
    - **Rekindling the Inner Flame:** In a quiet space, light a candle. Reflect on the wisdom gained from moments of darkness or challenge. Acknowledge your inner resilience and the enduring light of your **Inner Compass (Chapter II)**. This symbolizes the return of light and hope, even in the deepest night.
    - **Dream Work & Inner Journey:** Dedicate time to dream journaling and other practices that connect you to your subconscious, exploring the wisdom found in the depths, as outlined in **The Subconscious Oracle (Addendum II)**.

- **Storytelling by the Hearth:** Gather with your Hearth or loved ones to share stories of resilience, hope, and transformation, reinforcing **The Resonant Echo (Chapter VI)** and **The Living Chronicle (Addendum XIX)**.
- **Planning for the Return of Light:** While resting, gently begin to envision the intentions you wish to set for the coming spring, knowing that new growth will inevitably follow the deepest rest.

By consciously observing and participating in these **Seasonal Observances**, practitioners of **The Path of Unveiling** deepen their connection to **The Grand Tapestry (Chapter I)**, honor their own **Perpetual Becoming (Chapter IV)**, and find profound meaning in the natural rhythms of life.

Chapter X. Life Transitions - Rites of Passage

Life is a continuous unfolding, a series of passages from one state of being to another. Birth, maturity, partnership, significant achievements, and death are not mere events, but profound thresholds that mark shifts in identity, responsibility, and understanding. For millennia, cultures have recognized the importance of marking these **Life Transitions** with **Rites of Passage**—ceremonies and rituals that provide meaning, community support, and a framework for navigating change.

On **The Path of Unveiling**, we create and engage in secular Rites of Passage that honor these universal human experiences. These are not sacraments dictated by dogma, but conscious acts of acknowledgment, integration, and communal recognition. They serve to deepen our connection to **The Grand Tapestry (Chapter I)**, celebrate **The Perpetual Becoming (Chapter IV)**, and strengthen **The Architect of Self (Chapter V)** by providing a container for profound personal and collective transformation. They are a powerful expression of **The Resonant Echo (Chapter VI)**, connecting us to humanity's shared journey.

Each Rite of Passage, while unique in its specifics, shares common elements: a separation from the old, a liminal period of transformation, and a reincorporation into a new state of being.

I. Welcoming: The First Unveiling (Birth/Adoption)

- **Meaning:** The arrival of a new life into **The Grand Tapestry (Chapter I)**. It is a moment of profound joy, wonder, and the beginning of a unique **Perpetual Becoming (Chapter IV)**.
- **Purpose:** To officially welcome a new individual into the family and community of The Path. To acknowledge their inherent worth and potential, and for the community to affirm its support for the child's unfolding journey.
- **Practice:**
    - **Naming Ceremony:** A gathering where the child is formally named. Parents/guardians share the meaning behind the name and their hopes for the child's journey.
    - **Community Blessing:** Members of the Hearth or community offer non-dogmatic blessings, expressing wishes for the child's well-being, wisdom, and flourishing.
    - **Symbolic Gift:** A gift that symbolizes a core tenet of The Path (e.g., a small compass for **The Inner Compass**, a miniature loom for **The Grand Tapestry**) is presented to the child.

- **Commitment to Nurturing:** Parents/guardians and the community affirm their commitment to nurturing the child's **Inner Compass (Chapter II)**, fostering their **Responsibility and Agency (Chapter V)**, and supporting their **Perpetual Becoming (Chapter IV)**.

II. Unfolding: The Coming of Age (Adolescence/Young Adulthood)

- **Meaning:** The transition from childhood dependence to adult **Responsibility and Agency (Chapter V)**. A period of significant personal **Transformation and Growth (Chapter IV)**, self-discovery, and the development of one's **Inner Compass (Chapter II)**.
- **Purpose:** To acknowledge and celebrate an individual's emerging autonomy, their growing capacity for ethical judgment, and their readiness to take on greater responsibility within the community and the world.
- **Practice:**
    - **Personal Challenge/Quest:** The individual undertakes a self-chosen challenge that requires effort, resilience, and problem-solving (e.g., a solo journey, learning a complex skill, a significant community service project). This is an act of **The Architect of Self (Chapter V)**.
    - **Reflection & Declaration:** Upon completion, the individual reflects on their journey, articulating lessons learned, insights gained, and their personal

values. They then make a public declaration (within the Hearth) of their commitment to living by **The Ethical Compass (Chapter XI)** and contributing to **The Grand Tapestry (Chapter I)**. This becomes a part of their **Living Chronicle (Addendum XIX)**.
    - **Mentorship Acknowledgment:** The individual acknowledges mentors who have guided them (**The Guiding Hand - Addendum XVII**), and the community recognizes their new status as a contributing adult.

III. Weaving: Union and Partnership (Marriage/Committed Partnership)

- **Meaning:** The conscious choice to intertwine two individual paths into a shared journey, creating a new, stronger thread within **The Grand Tapestry (Chapter I)**. It symbolizes mutual commitment, shared growth, and the creation of a new, shared narrative.
- **Purpose:** To celebrate the union of two individuals, acknowledge their mutual commitment to **The Path**, and invite the community to witness and support their shared journey of **Perpetual Becoming (Chapter IV)**.
- **Practice:**
    - **Declaration of Intent:** Partners publicly declare their intentions, values, and commitments to each other, emphasizing mutual respect, **Compassion and Reason (Chapter XI)**, and shared growth.

- **Symbolic Weaving:** Partners might physically weave threads together, symbolizing the intertwining of their lives and the creation of a new, stronger fabric. This connects to **The Weave of Repair (Addendum XIII)** as a foundation for building strong relationships.
- **Community Affirmation:** The Hearth or community offers affirmations of support, recognizing the partners' contributions to **The Grand Tapestry (Chapter I)**.
- **Shared Visioning:** Partners articulate their shared vision for their future, their collective **Perpetual Becoming (Chapter IV)**, and how their union will contribute to the greater good. This also connects to **The Sacred Flame of Being (Addendum VIII)**, celebrating the holistic intimacy of their union.

IV. Passage: The Great Cycle (Death/Bereavement)

- **Meaning:** The ultimate **Life Transition**—the cessation of physical life and the profound shift in form. It is a moment of deep grief for those remaining, and a return of the individual's essence to **The Grand Tapestry (Chapter I)**. This is extensively explored in **Addendum IX: The Great Cycle**.
- **Purpose:** To honor the life lived, acknowledge the profound impact of the individual on the community, provide a space for communal grieving, and affirm the continuity of existence through transformation.

- **Practice:**
    - **Life Celebration:** A gathering focused on celebrating the life of the deceased. Stories are shared that highlight their unique journey, their contributions, and the **Resonant Echo (Chapter VI)** of their presence. This is a key part of **The Living Chronicle (Addendum XIX)**.
    - **Symbolic Release:** A ritual act to symbolize the release of the physical form while honoring the enduring connection (e.g., lighting candles, scattering ashes, planting a tree in their memory).
    - **Grief Sharing Circle:** A facilitated space for the community to share their grief, offer mutual support, and acknowledge the pain of loss, embodying **Compassion and Reason (Chapter XI)** and the principles of **The Weave of Repair (Addendum XIII)**.
    - **Affirmation of Continuity:** Acknowledging that while the physical form is gone, the individual's influence, love, and contribution remain woven into **The Grand Tapestry (Chapter I)** and continue to inspire **The Perpetual Becoming (Chapter IV)** of those they touched.

By consciously engaging with these **Rites of Passage**, practitioners of **The Path of Unveiling** navigate life's profound transitions with meaning, resilience, and the unwavering support of their community, transforming moments of change into opportunities for deeper **unveiling**.

Part 3: The Ethical Compass – Principles for a Flourishing Life

*To truly walk **The Path of Unveiling** is to live with integrity, compassion, and a conscious commitment to the well-being of oneself, others, and the interconnected world. Philosophy without ethical action remains abstract; wisdom without moral application lacks true power. **The Ethical Compass** provides a framework for navigating the complexities of human interaction and decision-making, grounding our principles in practical, actionable guidance.*

*This is not a rigid set of commandments, but a dynamic set of principles to be cultivated through **Reason** and applied with **Compassion**. It is a continuous process of discernment, reflection, and **Reasoned Error Correction**, guiding us to embody **The Architect of Self (Chapter V)** in service to **The Grand Tapestry (Chapter I)**.*

Chapter XI. Principles of The Ethical Compass

I. Compassion and Reason: The Guiding Lights

- **Principle:** All ethical decisions and actions on The Path are rooted in the dual pillars of **Compassion** (empathy, kindness, and a desire to alleviate suffering) and **Reason** (critical thinking, logical analysis, and an evidence-based approach to understanding reality).
- **Application:** Before acting, ask: "Is this choice compassionate towards all involved, including myself? Is it supported by reason and the best available understanding of the situation?"
- **Connection to Tenets:** These are the foundational qualities that illuminate **The Inner Compass (Chapter II)**. They are essential for navigating **The Weave of Repair (Addendum XIII)** and fostering **The Luminous Spark (Addendum XI)** through positive interactions.

II. Striving for Justice: The Equitable Weave

- **Principle:** Actively work towards fairness, equity, and the alleviation of suffering for all beings. Recognize and challenge systems of oppression, discrimination, and exploitation.
- **Application:** Support policies, practices, and individual actions that promote dignity, opportunity, and well-being for all, especially the vulnerable. Speak out against injustice when it is safe and effective to do so. This is a direct application of **The Architect of Self (Chapter V)** on a societal scale.
- **Connection to Tenets:** This principle directly strengthens **The Grand Tapestry (Chapter I)** by ensuring its threads are woven equitably. It is a continuous act of **Perpetual Becoming (Chapter IV)**, as societies constantly strive for greater justice. It is also central to **The Ethical Footprint (Addendum XVI)**.

III. Bodily Autonomy: The Sovereign Vessel

- **Principle:** Every individual has the inherent right to self-ownership and control over their own body, mind, and choices, free from coercion or undue influence. This extends to personal health, sexuality, and self-expression.
- **Application:** Respect the bodily autonomy of others, and assert your own with clarity. This includes enthusiastic consent in all interactions, as highlighted in **The Sacred Flame of Being (Addendum VIII)**.
- **Connection to Tenets:** This principle is foundational to **The Architect of Self (Chapter V)** and the cultivation of

The Inner Compass (Chapter II). It is also a core aspect of respecting **The Living Vessel (Addendum XII)**.

IV. Respect for Others' Freedoms: The Open Horizon

- **Principle:** Honor the right of others to hold their own beliefs, make their own choices, and pursue their own paths, provided those choices do not infringe upon the rights or well-being of others.
- **Application:** Engage in dialogue with an open mind, recognizing that diverse perspectives can enrich understanding. Avoid imposing your beliefs or values on others, as emphasized in the approach to **"The Great Unveiling"** and communication with varying faiths. This principle is crucial for embracing **The Wisdom of Humility (Addendum XV)**.
- **Connection to Tenets:** This directly supports **The Grand Tapestry (Chapter I)** by fostering a harmonious and diverse community. It is a practical application of **Balance and Harmony (Chapter III)** in interpersonal relations.

V. Reasoned Error Correction: The Path of Growth

- **Principle:** Acknowledge that all beings are fallible and that mistakes are inevitable. When errors occur, the ethical response is to take **Responsibility and Agency (Chapter V)**, learn from the experience, rectify any harm caused, and adjust one's understanding or behavior.

- **Application:** Practice self-compassion when you make mistakes, but also engage in honest self-assessment. Offer genuine apologies and make amends where appropriate. Be open to receiving constructive feedback from others without defensiveness. This is a core practice in **The Weave of Repair (Addendum XIII)**.
- **Connection to Tenets:** This principle is the engine of **The Perpetual Becoming (Chapter IV)**, transforming challenges into opportunities for growth. It strengthens **The Architect of Self (Chapter V)** through accountability and resilience. It also relies on **The Wisdom of Humility (Addendum XV)**.

VI. Scientific Understanding: The Unveiling of Reality

- **Principle:** Base one's understanding of the natural world and human experience on the best available evidence, critical inquiry, and the scientific method. Embrace curiosity and a willingness to revise beliefs in light of new discoveries.
- **Application:** Seek out reliable sources of information. Engage in lifelong learning about the universe, biology, psychology, and social dynamics. Value empirical evidence over superstition or unverified claims.
- **Connection to Tenets:** This principle is a direct pathway to **Gnosis** through rational inquiry, sharpening **The Inner Compass (Chapter II)**. It deeply informs our understanding of **The Grand Tapestry (Chapter I)** and **The Cosmic Reverence (Addendum XIV)**. It also supports

The Wisdom of Humility (Addendum XV) by acknowledging the provisional nature of scientific knowledge.

VII. Ethical Action: The Prevailing Spirit

- **Principle:** Ultimately, the principles of The Ethical Compass are not abstract rules but a living spirit that informs every choice and interaction. When faced with complex dilemmas, allow **Compassion and Reason** to guide your discernment, seeking the highest good for all involved.
- **Application:** Continuously reflect on how your actions embody these principles. Strive to live in alignment with your values, even when it is challenging. Let your life be a testament to the flourishing possible on The Path. This is the ultimate expression of **The Architect of Self (Chapter V)**.
- **Connection to Tenets:** This principle synthesizes all others, demonstrating how they are woven together to create a life of profound integrity and purpose. It is the active embodiment of **The Perpetual Becoming (Chapter IV)** and contributes directly to the well-being of **The Grand Tapestry (Chapter I)**.

By consciously integrating **The Ethical Compass** into daily life, practitioners of

The Path of Unveiling become agents of positive change, fostering harmony within themselves, their relationships, and the wider world, contributing to a more just, compassionate, and flourishing existence for all.

Part 4: Voices of Wisdom – An Anthology of Inspiration

The journey of **The Path of Unveiling** *is enriched by both direct experience and the accumulated wisdom of humanity. Throughout history, individuals and cultures have explored the profound questions of existence through diverse lenses—from the grand narratives of myth to the rigorous inquiries of science, from the contemplative depths of philosophy to the expressive power of art.*

This section, **Voices of Wisdom***, is an anthology—a curated collection of insights, perspectives, and expressions that resonate with the core tenets of The Path. It is not a prescriptive canon, but a vibrant library of human thought, designed to inspire, challenge, and deepen your* **Inner Compass (Chapter II)***. Here, we embrace the* **Resonant Echo (Chapter VI)***, recognizing that universal truths often appear in myriad forms, waiting to be unveiled.*

We approach these voices with **Reason and Compassion (Chapter XI)***, discerning their value not through dogmatic adherence, but through their capacity to illuminate our understanding of* **The Grand Tapestry (Chapter I)***, to guide our* **Perpetual Becoming (Chapter IV)***, and to empower us as* **Architects of Self (Chapter V)***. Whether ancient or modern, scientific or symbolic, these voices offer profound insights into the multifaceted nature of reality and the human spirit.*

Chapter XII. Mythological Archetypes - Secular Interpretation

*Myths are more than just ancient stories; they are the symbolic language of the human psyche, universal patterns of experience and meaning that resonate across cultures and throughout time. On **The Path of Unveiling**, we interpret **Mythological Archetypes** not as literal historical accounts, but as profound psychological and philosophical blueprints for understanding ourselves, our challenges, and our potential for **Transformation and Growth (Chapter IV)**. They are a powerful expression of **The Resonant Echo (Chapter VI)**.*

*By engaging with these archetypes, we gain insight into the universal patterns of **The Perpetual Becoming (Chapter IV)**, learn to navigate our own journeys with greater awareness, and connect to the shared narrative of humanity within **The Grand Tapestry (Chapter I)**.*

I. The Hero/Heroine's Journey (The Monomyth)

- **Archetype:** The universal pattern of adventure, transformation, and return found in countless myths, folk tales, and modern narratives.
- **Secular Interpretation:** This archetype is a metaphor for the individual's journey of **self-discovery and growth**. It represents the call to step outside one's comfort zone, face challenges, undergo a period of transformation, and return with new wisdom or gifts to share with the community. It is the quintessential story of **The Architect of Self (Chapter V)**.

- **Connection to The Path:**
    - **The Inner Compass (Chapter II):** The hero/heroine must ultimately trust their own intuition and inner guidance to navigate the trials.
    - **The Perpetual Becoming (Chapter IV):** The entire journey is one of continuous transformation, from an ordinary state to an enlightened one, often involving symbolic death and rebirth (**The Great Cycle - Addendum IX**).
    - **Responsibility and Agency (Chapter V):** The hero/heroine actively chooses to answer the call, faces obstacles with courage, and takes responsibility for their actions and their impact.
    - **The Living Chronicle (Addendum XIX):** Our own lives are unfolding hero/heroine's journeys, and by understanding this archetype, we can consciously shape our personal narratives.

II. The Wise Old Man/Woman (The Mentor)

- **Archetype:** A figure who provides guidance, wisdom, and often magical aid to the hero/heroine at crucial points in their journey. They represent accumulated knowledge and experience.
- **Secular Interpretation:** This archetype symbolizes the **universal human need for guidance and the value of mentorship**. It represents the wisdom gained through life experience, critical reflection, and the integration of knowledge. It can manifest as a literal mentor, a trusted elder, a profound book, or even an inner voice of wisdom.

- **Connection to The Path:**
    - **The Guiding Hand (Addendum XVII):** Directly embodies the role of **Unveilers** and **Keepers** in transmitting wisdom and supporting **Walkers** on their journeys.
    - **The Inner Compass (Chapter II):** While guiding, the mentor ultimately encourages the hero/heroine to trust their own inner wisdom, not to blindly follow.
    - **The Resonant Echo (Chapter VI):** Represents the timeless wisdom passed down through generations.

III. The Shadow (The Unacknowledged Self)

- **Archetype:** The repressed, unacknowledged, or undesirable aspects of the self—qualities, instincts, or experiences that the conscious ego has rejected or hidden.
- **Secular Interpretation:** This archetype represents the psychological concept of the subconscious or unconscious mind, containing aspects of ourselves we fear or deny. Integrating the shadow is crucial for psychological wholeness, **Balance and Harmony (Chapter III)**, and genuine self-acceptance.

- **Connection to The Path:**
    - **The Scales of Being (Chapter III):** Integrating the shadow is a key aspect of balancing light and dark within the self, moving towards psychological wholeness.
    - **The Inner Compass (Chapter II):** Confronting the shadow can lead to profound **Gnosis** about one's true motivations and hidden potentials.
    - **The Weave of Repair (Addendum XIII):** Acknowledging one's own shadow aspects can be crucial for understanding and resolving internal and interpersonal conflicts.
    - **The Sacred Flame of Being (Addendum VIII):** Often, societal or religious shame around sexuality can push aspects of our authentic sexual self into the shadow, requiring conscious integration.

IV. The Trickster (The Catalyst of Change)

- **Archetype:** A mischievous, often boundary-crossing figure who disrupts norms, challenges authority, and uses wit or deception to expose truths or facilitate change. They are often paradoxical figures—both creative and destructive.
- **Secular Interpretation:** This archetype symbolizes the **power of disruption, humor, and unconventional thinking** to break stagnant patterns. The Trickster reminds us not to take ourselves or established systems too seriously, and that innovation often comes from challenging the status quo. They embody the dynamic aspect of **The Perpetual Becoming (Chapter IV)**.

- **Connection to The Path:**
    - **The Luminous Spark (Addendum XI):** Directly embodies the role of humor and play in challenging rigidity and fostering adaptability.
    - **The Wisdom of Humility (Addendum XV):** The Trickster often exposes the flaws in rigid certainty, encouraging us to embrace doubt and the unknown.
    - **Reasoned Error Correction (Chapter XI):** The Trickster's disruptions can force us to confront our mistakes and adapt our approaches.

V. The Great Mother/Father (The Nurturing/Structuring Principle)

- **Archetype:** Universal figures representing the nurturing, life-giving, and sustaining aspects of existence (Mother) and the structuring, ordering, and protective aspects (Father). These are not gender-specific but energetic principles.
- **Secular Interpretation:** These archetypes symbolize the **fundamental forces of creation, sustenance, and order** in the universe and within ourselves. The "Great Mother" can represent nature, intuition, and unconditional acceptance, while the "Great Father" can represent reason, structure, and ethical boundaries.

- **Connection to The Path:**
    - **The Grand Tapestry (Chapter I):** Represents the fundamental forces that weave and sustain all existence.
    - **The Scales of Being (Chapter III):** Emphasizes the need for **Balance and Harmony** between nurturing and structuring principles within ourselves and our communities. This connects to the rediscovery of the **Sacred Feminine (Addendum VIII)**.
    - **The Ethical Compass (Chapter XI):** Can be seen as embodying both the compassion (Mother) and reason/justice (Father) principles.

By exploring these and other **Mythological Archetypes**, practitioners of The Path of Unveiling gain a deeper understanding of the universal patterns that shape human experience, enriching their **Inner Compass (Chapter II)** and guiding their **Perpetual Becoming (Chapter IV)** within **The Grand Tapestry (Chapter I)**.

Chapter XIII. Philosophical Excerpts

*Philosophy, literally "the love of wisdom," has been humanity's enduring quest to understand existence, knowledge, values, reason, mind, and language. Unlike myth, which often speaks in symbols, philosophy directly engages with concepts through logical inquiry and critical thought. On **The Path of Unveiling**, we draw from **Philosophical Excerpts** that resonate with our core tenets, offering intellectual frameworks and profound insights that deepen **The Inner Compass (Chapter II)** and strengthen **The Architect of Self (Chapter V)**. These voices contribute to **The Resonant Echo (Chapter VI)**, demonstrating humanity's continuous pursuit of understanding.*

I. Stoicism (Ancient Greece/Rome)

- **Core Idea:** Focus on what is within your control (your thoughts, actions, reactions) and accept what is not. Cultivate virtue, reason, and inner tranquility regardless of external circumstances.
- **Relevance to The Path:**
    - **Responsibility and Agency (The Architect of Self - Chapter V):** Stoicism is a powerful guide for taking

full ownership of one's internal state and choices, even in difficult situations. It empowers the individual to consciously shape their character.
    - **Balance and Harmony (The Scales of Being - Chapter III):** Cultivating equanimity and emotional resilience through rational thought, finding balance between passion and reason.
    - **The River of Now (Addendum X):** Emphasizes living fully in the present moment and accepting the flow of events, rather than dwelling on the past or worrying excessively about the future.
    - **The Ethical Compass (Chapter XI):** Virtue and reason are central to Stoic ethics, aligning with **Compassion and Reason** as guiding lights.
- **Excerpt Example (Seneca):** "We suffer more often in imagination than in reality."
    - **Reflection:** How does this thought encourage you to focus your **Agency** on your internal reactions rather than external events? How does it relate to cultivating **The Inner Compass**?

II. Existentialism (19th-20th Century Europe)

- **Core Idea:** Existence precedes essence. We are born without inherent meaning or purpose, and it is our responsibility to create our own meaning through our choices and actions. Emphasizes freedom, responsibility, and the burden of choice.
- **Relevance to The Path:**

- - **Responsibility and Agency (The Architect of Self - Chapter V):** Directly aligns with the core idea that we are the architects of our own lives, responsible for defining our values and purpose.
  - **The Wisdom of Humility (Addendum XV):** Embraces the inherent uncertainty and lack of pre-ordained meaning in the universe, requiring courage to create one's own path.
  - **The Perpetual Becoming (Chapter IV):** Life is an ongoing process of self-creation through choices, reflecting continuous transformation.
- **Excerpt Example (Jean-Paul Sartre):** "Man is condemned to be free; because once thrown into the world, he is responsible for everything he does."
  - **Reflection:** How does this idea empower you to take full **Responsibility and Agency** for your choices? What does it mean to be free to define your own purpose on **The Path**?

III. Humanism (Ancient to Modern)

- **Core Idea:** Emphasizes human values, capabilities, and reason. Focuses on human flourishing, ethics, and progress through human effort, rather than divine intervention. Often secular or non-theistic.
- **Relevance to The Path:**
  - **The Ethical Compass (Chapter XI):** Humanism provides a strong foundation for secular ethics,

prioritizing human well-being, justice, and compassion through rational inquiry.
    - **Responsibility and Agency (The Architect of Self - Chapter V):** Places the burden and opportunity of creating a better world squarely on human shoulders.
    - **The Grand Tapestry (Chapter I):** Fosters a deep appreciation for human interconnectedness and the collective human project of progress.
    - **The Cosmic Reverence (Addendum XIV):** Finds profound awe and wonder in human potential, creativity, and the natural world.
- **Excerpt Example (Protagoras):** "Man is the measure of all things."
    - **Reflection:** How does this ancient Greek humanistic idea resonate with the Path's emphasis on individual **Gnosis** and **The Inner Compass** as guides for understanding reality?

IV. Taoism (Ancient China)

- **Core Idea:** Living in harmony with the *Tao*, the natural, unnamable, underlying order of the universe. Emphasizes spontaneity, simplicity, effortless action (*Wu Wei*), and the balance of opposites.
- **Relevance to The Path:**
    - **The Grand Tapestry (Chapter I):** The Tao is the ultimate expression of the interconnectedness of all being.

- - **Balance and Harmony (The Scales of Being - Chapter III):** The concept of Yin and Yang is central to Taoism, illustrating dynamic equilibrium.
  - **The River of Now (Addendum X):** Emphasizes flowing with the natural rhythms of life and accepting change, rather than resisting it.
  - **The Luminous Spark (Addendum XI):** Encourages a playful, spontaneous approach to life, finding joy in simplicity.
- **Excerpt Example (Lao Tzu, Tao Te Ching):** "The softest thing in the world overcomes the hardest thing in the world."
  - **Reflection:** How does this paradoxical statement relate to finding strength in adaptability and gentleness, aligning with **The Scales of Being** and **The Perpetual Becoming (Chapter IV)**?

V. Process Philosophy (Modern)

- **Core Idea:** Reality is fundamentally about processes, change, and becoming, rather than static substances or fixed entities. Everything is in a state of flux and interconnectedness.
- **Relevance to The Path:**
  - **The Perpetual Becoming (Chapter IV):** Directly aligns with the core tenet that transformation and growth are constant and inherent to existence.

- **The Grand Tapestry (Chapter I):** Emphasizes the dynamic, relational nature of all things, where entities are defined by their interactions and changes.
- **The River of Now (Addendum X):** Highlights the continuous flow of time and the importance of engaging with the present moment as the site of all becoming.

- **Excerpt Example (Heraclitus, Pre-Socratic):** "No man ever steps in the same river twice, for it's not the same river and he's not the same man."
  - **Reflection:** How does this ancient insight, foundational to process philosophy, illuminate your understanding of **The Perpetual Becoming** in your own life?

By engaging with these and other **Philosophical Excerpts**, practitioners of The Path of Unveiling sharpen their critical thinking, broaden their perspectives, and find intellectual resonance for their journey of **unveiling** the profound truths of existence.

Chapter XIV. Scientific Insights

Science, at its heart, is a systematic approach to **unveiling** *the nature of reality through observation, experimentation, and critical analysis. Far from being antithetical to a meaningful life, scientific understanding offers profound insights into the workings of the universe, the intricacies of life, and the complexities of the human mind. On* **The Path of Unveiling***, we embrace* **Scientific Insights** *as a powerful lens through which to deepen our* **Inner Compass (Chapter II)***, understand* **The Grand Tapestry (Chapter I)***, and guide our* **Perpetual Becoming (Chapter IV)***. These insights are a crucial part of* **The Resonant Echo (Chapter VI)***, representing humanity's collective, evidence-based wisdom.*

By integrating scientific understanding, we ground our journey in verifiable knowledge, fostering **Reason (Chapter XI)** *and cultivating* **The Wisdom of Humility (Addendum XV)** *by acknowledging the provisional nature of even our most advanced understandings.*

I. Cosmology: Our Cosmic Origin and Place

- **Core Idea:** The study of the origin, evolution, and large-scale structure of the universe. Modern cosmology, through theories like the Big Bang, reveals a universe of immense scale, dynamic evolution, and fundamental interconnectedness.
- **Relevance to The Path:**
    - **The Grand Tapestry (Chapter I):** Cosmology provides the ultimate context for **The Grand Tapestry**, showing how all matter and energy originated from a singular event and has been evolving for billions of years. The fact that the elements composing our bodies were forged in stars (stellar nucleosynthesis) offers a profound, literal connection to the cosmos, as explored in **Addendum I: The Cosmic Tapestry**.
    - **The Perpetual Becoming (Chapter IV):** The universe itself is in a constant state of **Transformation and Growth**, from the formation of galaxies to the life cycles of stars.
    - **The Cosmic Reverence (Addendum XIV):** Understanding the vastness and complexity of the universe naturally evokes profound awe and wonder, a secular form of reverence for existence.
- **Insight Example:** "We are a way for the cosmos to know itself." (Carl Sagan)
    - **Reflection:** How does the scientific understanding of our cosmic origins deepen your sense of belonging within **The Grand Tapestry** and inspire **The Cosmic Reverence**?

II. Evolutionary Biology: The Dance of Life

- **Core Idea:** The study of how life on Earth has changed over vast timescales through processes like natural selection, adaptation, and speciation. It reveals the deep interconnectedness of all living things and their continuous adaptation.
- **Relevance to The Path:**
    - **The Perpetual Becoming (Chapter IV):** Evolution is the quintessential example of **Transformation and Growth**, demonstrating life's ceaseless drive to adapt and diversify.
    - **The Grand Tapestry (Chapter I):** All life forms are interconnected through common ancestry and ecological relationships, forming a vast, intricate web of interdependence. This understanding informs **The Ethical Footprint (Addendum XVI)**.
    - **The Living Vessel (Addendum XII):** Our own bodies are products of billions of years of evolution, embodying incredible resilience and adaptive wisdom.
- **Insight Example:** The concept of *common descent*, meaning all life on Earth shares a common ancestor.
    - **Reflection:** How does recognizing your shared ancestry with all life on Earth deepen your sense of connection to **The Grand Tapestry** and foster **Compassion (Chapter XI)** for other living beings?

III. Neuroscience and Psychology: The Mind Unveiled

- **Core Idea:** The study of the brain and nervous system, and the scientific study of mind and behavior. These fields provide insights into consciousness, emotion, decision-making, and the mechanisms of personal growth.
- **Relevance to The Path:**
    - **The Inner Compass (Chapter II):** Neuroscience explores the biological basis of intuition, mindfulness, and emotional regulation, providing a scientific understanding of how to cultivate **Inner Wisdom**.
    - **The Architect of Self (Chapter V):** Concepts like *neuroplasticity* (the brain's ability to change and adapt) provide scientific validation for our **Responsibility and Agency** in shaping our thoughts, habits, and ultimately, our selves. This is central to **The Wellspring Within (Addendum XVIII)**.
    - **Balance and Harmony (The Scales of Being - Chapter III):** Understanding brain chemistry and the interplay of different brain regions helps us comprehend the biological basis of emotional and mental balance.
    - **The Subconscious Oracle (Addendum II):** Neuroscience and psychology provide frameworks for understanding the workings of the

subconscious mind and its influence on our conscious experience.
- **Insight Example:** The discovery of *mirror neurons*, which fire both when an individual performs an action and when they observe the same action performed by another, providing a neurological basis for empathy.
    - **Reflection:** How does this scientific understanding of empathy reinforce the principle of **Compassion (Chapter XI)** and our inherent connection within **The Grand Tapestry?**

IV. Systems Theory and Ecology: Interconnectedness in Action

- **Core Idea:** The study of systems—collections of interconnected parts that form a complex whole. Ecology, in particular, examines the intricate relationships between living organisms and their environment.
- **Relevance to The Path:**
    - **The Grand Tapestry (Chapter I):** Systems theory provides a rigorous framework for understanding the profound interconnectedness of all things, from ecosystems to social structures.
    - **The Ethical Footprint (Addendum XVI):** Ecological principles directly inform our understanding of sustainability and the far-reaching consequences of our actions on complex systems, emphasizing our **Responsibility and Agency (Chapter V).**
    - **Balance and Harmony (The Scales of Being - Chapter III):** Healthy systems are characterized by

dynamic balance and feedback loops that maintain equilibrium.
- **Insight Example:** The *butterfly effect* in chaos theory, where a small change in one part of a complex system can lead to large, unpredictable changes elsewhere.
  - **Reflection:** How does this illustrate the profound impact of individual actions within **The Grand Tapestry**, even seemingly small ones?

By continuously engaging with **Scientific Insights**, practitioners of The Path of Unveiling cultivate a rational yet awe-filled understanding of reality. This evidence-based approach strengthens **The Inner Compass (Chapter II)**, empowers **The Architect of Self (Chapter V)**, and deepens our reverence for the magnificent, ever-unfolding **Grand Tapestry (Chapter I)** of existence.

Chapter XV. Poetry and Art

Beyond the logical structures of philosophy and the empirical observations of science, humanity has always sought to express and understand reality through the evocative power of **Poetry and Art**. *These forms of expression tap into the depths of emotion, intuition, and imagination, speaking a universal language that transcends cultural barriers and intellectual frameworks. On* **The Path of Unveiling**, *we recognize* **Poetry and Art** *as profound manifestations of* **The Resonant Echo (Chapter VI)**, *offering unique pathways to* **Gnosis** *and enriching our experience of* **The Grand Tapestry (Chapter I)**.

By engaging with art and poetry, we cultivate **The Luminous Spark (Addendum XI)**, *find* **Balance and Harmony (Chapter III)** *in the interplay of beauty and truth, and discover new dimensions of our* **Inner Compass (Chapter II)**. *These creative expressions serve as a vital counterpoint to purely rational inquiry, reminding us of the multifaceted nature of human experience.*

I. Poetry: The Language of the Soul

- **Core Idea:** Poetry uses rhythm, imagery, metaphor, and evocative language to convey complex emotions, profound insights, and the ineffable aspects of human experience that prose often struggles to capture.
- **Relevance to The Path:**
    - **The Resonant Echo (Chapter VI):** Poetry is a direct channel for universal human experiences—love, loss, joy, wonder, grief (**The Great Cycle - Addendum IX**), and transformation (**The Perpetual Becoming - Chapter IV**).
    - **The Inner Compass (Chapter II):** By engaging with poetry, we can access intuitive understanding and emotional resonance that deepens our personal **Gnosis**.
    - **The Living Chronicle (Addendum XIX):** Poetry can be a powerful medium for crafting and expressing one's **Personal Narrative**, capturing moments of **unveiling**.
    - **The Cosmic Reverence (Addendum XIV):** Many poems evoke a sense of awe and wonder at the natural world and the cosmos.
- **Example (Rumi):** "The wound is the place where the Light enters you."
    - **Reflection:** How does this poetic insight resonate with **The Perpetual Becoming (Chapter IV)**, suggesting that challenges and pain can be catalysts for growth and the **unveiling** of inner light?

II. Visual Arts: The Canvas of Perception

- **Core Idea:** Painting, sculpture, photography, and other visual arts offer unique perspectives on reality, allowing us to see the world through another's eyes, explore abstract concepts, and evoke powerful emotions without words.
- **Relevance to The Path:**
    - **The Grand Tapestry (Chapter I):** Visual art can capture and express the intricate beauty and interconnectedness of the natural world, human relationships, and cosmic phenomena.
    - **The Living Vessel (Addendum XII):** Art can explore the human form, movement, and sensory experience, deepening our appreciation for the body.
    - **The Cosmic Reverence (Addendum XIV):** Many artworks inspire awe and wonder through their scale, detail, or the profound ideas they represent.
    - **The Luminous Spark (Addendum XI):** Engaging with art can be a source of pure joy, inspiration, and creative stimulation.
- **Example (Vincent van Gogh, *The Starry Night*):** Depicts a swirling, vibrant night sky with an expressive cypress tree.
    - **Reflection:** How does this painting evoke a sense of the dynamic, ever-changing nature of the universe (**The Perpetual Becoming - Chapter IV**) and inspire

The Cosmic Reverence (Addendum XIV), even in its abstract representation?

III. Music: The Universal Language of Emotion

- **Core Idea:** Music, through rhythm, melody, and harmony, communicates directly with our emotions and subconscious, often bypassing intellectual filters. It can evoke a vast spectrum of feelings, from profound sorrow to ecstatic joy.
- **Relevance to The Path:**
    - **The Resonant Echo (Chapter VI):** Music is a primal form of human expression, resonating with universal emotions and experiences across all cultures.
    - **Balance and Harmony (The Scales of Being - Chapter III):** Music is inherently about balance, tension, and resolution, mirroring the dynamic equilibrium we seek in life.
    - **The Luminous Spark (Addendum XI):** Music can be a powerful source of joy, inspiration, and emotional release.
    - **The Inner Compass (Chapter II):** Listening mindfully to music can facilitate introspection and access deeper emotional truths.
- **Example (Ludwig van Beethoven, Symphony No. 9):** Particularly the "Ode to Joy" movement.
    - **Reflection:** How does this music evoke a sense of universal connection and shared human

experience, reflecting **The Grand Tapestry (Chapter I)** and inspiring **The Luminous Spark (Addendum XI)**?

IV. Performance Arts: Embodied Storytelling

- **Core Idea:** Dance, theater, and other performance arts use the human body, voice, and movement to tell stories, explore emotions, and create shared experiences that resonate deeply with audiences.
- **Relevance to The Path:**
    - **The Living Vessel (Addendum XII):** Performance arts celebrate the body as a powerful instrument of expression and communication.
    - **The Living Chronicle (Addendum XIX):** They are dynamic forms of storytelling, bringing narratives to life and creating shared communal experiences.
    - **The Weave of Repair (Addendum XIII):** Performance can be a powerful tool for exploring conflict, empathy, and reconciliation through dramatic representation.
    - **The Perpetual Becoming (Chapter IV):** Performances are inherently transient, evolving in the **Eternal Now (Addendum X)**, reflecting the dynamic nature of existence.

By engaging with **Poetry and Art** in their myriad forms, practitioners of The Path of Unveiling cultivate a richer, more nuanced understanding of reality. They learn to perceive the world not just through logic, but through the profound language of beauty, emotion, and symbolic meaning, deepening their **Gnosis** and enriching their journey of **unveiling**.

Chapter XVI. Gnostic Fragments - Reinterpreted

The ancient Gnostic traditions, flourishing in the early centuries CE, offered a radical departure from conventional religious thought. Explored mainly through early Christian mysticism, their core emphasis was on Gnosis—direct, experiential knowledge or insight—as the path to understanding reality and liberation, rather than through faith in external dogma. While often couched in complex mythological narratives and dualistic cosmologies, the psychological and philosophical insights within **Gnostic Fragments** *offer profound metaphorical tools for* **The Path of Unveiling***.*

On The Path, we approach these fragments not as literal religious texts, but as rich **Symbolic Language (Chapter XVII)***. We re-interpret their concepts through a secular, psychological, and philosophical lens, recognizing them as powerful expressions of* **The Resonant Echo (Chapter VI)***. They provide allegories for the inner journey, the nature of consciousness, and the process of self-discovery, deepening our* **Inner Compass (Chapter II)** *and guiding our* **Perpetual Becoming (Chapter IV)***.*

I. The Pleroma (The Fullness / Wholeness)

- **Gnostic Concept:** The Pleroma is the divine totality, the ultimate source of all being, a realm of perfect light, truth, and wholeness from which emanations (Aeons) descend.
- **Secular Reinterpretation:** Metaphorically, the Pleroma represents the **fullness of potential within consciousness**, the ultimate state of psychological integration and wholeness that we strive for. It is the inherent, complete nature of reality before it is fragmented by limited perception. It can also be seen as the unified field of **The Grand Tapestry (Chapter I)**, the interconnected whole from which all individual experiences arise.
- **Connection to The Path:**
    - **The Inner Compass (Chapter II):** The pursuit of **Gnosis** is the journey back to this inner fullness, recognizing the inherent wisdom and completeness within.
    - **Balance and Harmony (The Scales of Being - Chapter III):** The Pleroma represents a state of perfect balance and integration of all aspects of being.
    - **The Cosmic Reverence (Addendum XIV):** It evokes a sense of awe at the vast, unified nature of existence.

II. The Demiurge (The Imperfect Creator / The Ego)

- **Gnostic Concept:** An imperfect, often ignorant, lesser deity who created the material world, mistakenly believing himself to be the supreme God. This world, therefore, is flawed and a prison for the divine spark.
- **Secular Reinterpretation:** The Demiurge can be seen as a powerful metaphor for the **ego-mind**—that part of our consciousness that creates our personal reality, often believing itself to be the ultimate authority. This ego, while necessary for navigating the material world, can also create illusions of separation, suffering, and limitation if it is not aligned with the deeper wisdom of **The Inner Compass (Chapter II)**. It represents the limitations of our individual perception within **The Grand Tapestry (Chapter I)**.
- **Connection to The Path:**
    - **The Architect of Self (Chapter V):** Understanding the "Demiurge" as the ego helps us to consciously direct our **Responsibility and Agency**, recognizing when our ego's desires might be out of alignment with our higher purpose.
    - **The Wisdom of Humility (Addendum XV):** Acknowledging the "imperfection" of the ego's creation fosters humility and openness to other perspectives.
    - **Reasoned Error Correction (Chapter XI):** The Demiurge's "mistakes" serve as a metaphor for our own errors in judgment, prompting us to learn and correct our course.

III. The Divine Spark / Aeons (The Inner Light / Aspects of Consciousness)

- **Gnostic Concept:** Fragments of the divine light (Pleroma) trapped within the material bodies created by the Demiurge. These are the true essence of humanity, seeking to return to their source. Aeons are divine emanations or aspects of the Pleroma.
- **Secular Reinterpretation:** The "Divine Spark" represents our **inherent potential for consciousness, wisdom, and connection to the universal**. It is the innate capacity for **Gnosis** within each individual. The "Aeons" can be seen as different facets or qualities of consciousness that we cultivate and integrate on our journey of **Perpetual Becoming (Chapter IV)**. This is the **Sacred Flame of Being (Addendum VIII)** within each of us.
- **Connection to The Path:**
    - **The Inner Compass (Chapter II):** The "spark" is our innate guide, constantly seeking to unveil deeper truths.
    - **The Perpetual Becoming (Chapter IV):** The journey of "returning to the Pleroma" is the process of continuous self-actualization and integration.
    - **The Luminous Spark (Addendum XI):** Directly relates to the cultivation of joy, creativity, and inner light.

IV. The Awakening / Remembrance (Gnosis as Unveiling)

- **Gnostic Concept:** The process by which the divine spark within recognizes its true origin and nature, gaining **Gnosis** and thereby achieving liberation from the material world's illusions.
- **Secular Reinterpretation:** This is the core process of **unveiling** on The Path. It is the **conscious awakening** to our deeper self, our interconnectedness, and our capacity for **Responsibility and Agency (Chapter V)**. It is a process of "remembering" inherent truths that have been obscured by conditioning or limited perception. This direct experience of insight is **Gnosis**.
- **Connection to The Path:**
  - **The Pursuit of Gnosis (Chapter II):** This is the central aim of The Path—experiential knowing.
  - **The Perpetual Becoming (Chapter IV):** Awakening is not a single event but a continuous process of deepening insight and transformation.
  - **The Living Chronicle (Addendum XIX):** Each "awakening" or "remembrance" becomes a significant chapter in one's **Personal Narrative**.

By re-interpreting **Gnostic Fragments** through a secular, psychological, and philosophical lens, practitioners of The Path of Unveiling gain powerful allegories for their inner journey. These ancient voices, stripped of their dogmatic interpretations, become profound tools for self-reflection, deepening **The Inner Compass (Chapter II)**, and illuminating the path of **Perpetual Becoming (Chapter IV)** towards greater wholeness and awareness.

Chapter XVII. Symbolic Language - Tarot, Runes, & Astrology as Tools

*Humanity's quest for meaning has often led to the creation of intricate systems of **Symbolic Language**—visual, numerical, and archetypal frameworks that offer a different way of understanding ourselves and the world. Systems like Tarot, Runes, and Astrology, while historically used for divination or literal prediction, can be re-interpreted on **The Path of Unveiling** as powerful, secular tools for introspection, self-reflection, and pattern recognition.*

*We approach these systems not as sources of external prophecy or dogma, but as profound expressions of **The Resonant Echo (Chapter VI)**. They offer a rich vocabulary of archetypes and metaphors that speak to our subconscious, helping us to clarify **The Inner Compass (Chapter II)**, process our experiences, and gain new perspectives on our **Perpetual Becoming (Chapter IV)**. They are a means to engage with **The Subconscious Oracle (Addendum II)**, providing a mirror for our inner landscape.*

*By engaging with these symbolic languages, we cultivate **The Wisdom of Humility (Addendum XV)**, recognizing that* *their power lies in their capacity to stimulate our own intuition and insight, rather than providing definitive answers. They are tools for **unveiling**, not for foretelling.*

I. Tarot: The Archetypal Journey in Cards

- **Core Idea:** A deck of 78 cards, each with rich symbolic imagery, traditionally used for divination. On The Path, it is re-interpreted as a **psychological and narrative tool** that reflects the archetypal journey of human experience.
- **Secular Reinterpretation:** Each card represents a universal theme, a stage of life, an emotional state, or an archetypal character. A "reading" becomes a structured method for self-reflection, allowing the individual to project their current situation onto the cards and gain new perspectives or frame their **Personal Narrative (Addendum XIX)**. It helps in understanding the interplay of different forces in one's life, aligning with **The Scales of Being (Chapter III)**.
- **Connection to The Path:**
    - **The Resonant Echo (Chapter VI):** Tarot cards are rich in universal symbols and archetypes (e.g., The Fool's Journey as a metaphor for **The Hero/Heroine's Journey - Chapter XII**).
    - **The Inner Compass (Chapter II):** Used as a prompt for intuition and self-reflection, helping to access **Gnosis**.
    - **The Architect of Self (Chapter V):** Provides insights into personal challenges and

opportunities, empowering conscious choice and **Responsibility and Agency**.
    - **The Living Chronicle (Addendum XIX):** Can help individuals articulate and understand the unfolding story of their lives.
- **Practice Example:** Draw a single card at the start of the day. Reflect on its imagery and traditional meaning. How might this archetype or theme play out in your day? Use it as a lens for mindful observation, connecting to **The River of Now (Addendum X)**.

II. Runes: Ancient Symbols of Insight

- **Core Idea:** Ancient Germanic and Norse alphabetic characters, each with a specific symbolic meaning, traditionally carved onto wood or stone and used for divination or magical purposes.
- **Secular Reinterpretation:** Each Rune represents a specific concept, force, or aspect of the natural world and human experience (e.g., *Fehu* for wealth/abundance, *Uruz* for strength/wildness, *Laguz* for water/flow). A "casting" becomes a method for focused contemplation, allowing the individual to draw symbolic insights related to a question or situation. They are a way to engage with the **Resonant Echo (Chapter VI)** of ancient wisdom.
- **Connection to The Path:**
    - **The Grand Tapestry (Chapter I):** Many runes are deeply connected to natural elements and cycles,

reinforcing our connection to the Earth and its energies.
- **The Inner Compass (Chapter II):** Provides a framework for intuitive understanding and self-reflection, particularly useful for understanding challenges and opportunities.
- **The Perpetual Becoming (Chapter IV):** Runes can symbolize stages of growth, transformation, and the dynamic interplay of forces in life.
- **The Wisdom of Humility (Addendum XV):** Encourages an open mind to the subtle messages and patterns in life, without seeking definitive answers.
- **Practice Example:** Hold a question in your mind and draw one or three runes. Reflect on the symbolic meaning of the drawn runes. How do these concepts relate to your question or current situation? What insight do they offer for your **Architect of Self (Chapter V)**?

III. Astrology: Cosmic Patterns as Personal Archetypes

- **Core Idea:** The study of the positions and movements of celestial bodies and their supposed influence on human affairs and the natural world. Traditionally used for predicting events or understanding personality.
- **Secular Reinterpretation:** Astrology is viewed as a complex **symbolic language** and a psychological framework. The planets, zodiac signs, and houses represent universal archetypes, psychological drives, and

areas of life experience. A birth chart becomes a "map of potential"—a snapshot of inherent psychological tendencies and life themes at the moment of birth. It is a tool for self-understanding and exploring the interplay of various aspects of personality, not a deterministic prophecy. This is a profound expression of **The Resonant Echo (Chapter VI)**.

- **Connection to The Path:**
    - **The Architect of Self (Chapter V)**: Provides insights into inherent strengths, challenges, and patterns, empowering individuals to consciously work with their predispositions.
    - **The Scales of Being (Chapter III)**: Helps in understanding the dynamic interplay of different psychological energies within oneself, fostering **Balance and Harmony**.
    - **The Grand Tapestry (Chapter I)**: Connects the individual to the larger cosmic patterns, fostering **The Cosmic Reverence (Addendum XIV)**.
    - **The Perpetual Becoming (Chapter IV)**: Astrological transits can be seen as symbolic indicators of periods of **Transformation and Growth**, inviting conscious engagement with life's cycles.
- **Practice Example:** Research the archetypal meaning of your sun sign, moon sign, or rising sign. How do these symbolic descriptions resonate with your own personality and experiences? How can understanding these archetypes help you to better direct your **Responsibility**

and Agency (Chapter V)? This is also relevant to **Chapter VIII. Weekly & Monthly Cycles**, which references planetary influences.

By engaging with these and other **Symbolic Languages**, practitioners of The Path of Unveiling unlock a deeper, intuitive understanding of themselves and the world. They learn to read the subtle patterns of existence, access the wisdom of **The Subconscious Oracle (Addendum II)**, and navigate their journey of **unveiling** with greater insight, creativity, and a profound appreciation for the multifaceted ways meaning is expressed in **The Grand Tapestry (Chapter I)**.

Part 5: The Continuing Chronicle

This Chronicle, which you hold in your hands, is not a finished book. It is, in essence, a living document—a snapshot of **The Path of Unveiling** *as it stands now, informed by ancient wisdom, modern understanding, and the collective human journey. But the true power of The Path lies not in its written words, but in its lived experience.*

The Continuing Chronicle *is the unfolding narrative of every individual who walks this Path, every Hearth that gathers, and every moment of* **Gnosis** *that illuminates a new truth. It is the ongoing* **Perpetual Becoming (Chapter IV)** *of a conscious humanity, weaving new threads into* **The Grand Tapestry (Chapter I)** *of existence.*

I. The Living Text

*The principles, practices, and insights contained within these pages are not static. They are dynamic tools, meant to be engaged with, tested, refined, and expanded upon through your own experience. Just as science continually **unveils** new layers of reality (**Chapter XIV. Scientific Insights**), and philosophy evolves with new thought (**Chapter XIII. Philosophical Excerpts**), so too does The Path deepen and broaden with each practitioner's journey.*

*Consider this Chronicle as a foundational map, but remember that the territory itself is vast and ever-changing. Your own life, your own insights, your own challenges and triumphs, are the next chapters waiting to be written. Your **Personal Narrative (Addendum XIX)** is a vital contribution to this living text.*

II. Your Role in The Continuing Chronicle

As you embark upon or continue your journey on **The Path of Unveiling**, you become an active participant in **The Continuing Chronicle**. Your **Responsibility and Agency (Chapter V)** are paramount.

- **Embody The Path:** Live the principles of **The Ethical Compass (Chapter XI)** with **Compassion and Reason**. Integrate the daily, weekly, and seasonal practices (**Part 2**) into your life. Nurture **The Wellspring Within (Addendum XVIII)** through self-care.

- **Cultivate Your Inner Compass:** Continuously seek **Gnosis** through introspection, mindfulness (**Chapter VII. Daily Practices**), and engagement with the world. Embrace **The Wisdom of Humility (Addendum XV)**, recognizing that the journey of **unveiling** is infinite.

- **Share Your Unveilings:** When appropriate and with integrity, share your insights, experiences, and lessons learned with your Hearth and fellow travelers. Your unique **Personal Narrative (Addendum XIX)** contributes to **The Resonant Echo (Chapter VI)**, providing guidance and inspiration for others. This is a core aspect of **The Guiding Hand (Addendum XVII)**.

- **Contribute to The Grand Tapestry:** Engage actively in your community and the wider world, applying the principles of **Conscious Consumption and Stewardship (Addendum XVI)** and working towards **The Weave of Repair (Addendum XIII)** where needed.

- **Nurture The Hearth:** If you feel called, consider taking on the role of a **Keeper** or **Unveiler**, helping to facilitate and guide others on their journeys (**Chapter X. Life Transitions - Rites of Passage** and **Addendum VI: The Council of Unveilers**).

The Path of Unveiling is not a destination, but a courageous and compassionate way of walking through life. It is an invitation to embrace the mystery, to find meaning in the mundane, and to contribute your unique light to the **Grand Tapestry (Chapter I)**. May your journey be filled with profound unveilings, deep connection, and the boundless joy of **Perpetual Becoming (Chapter IV)**.

Glossary of Terms

This glossary defines the core specialized terms used throughout *The Chronicle of The Path of Unveiling*. It is designed to provide clarity for new readers and serve as a consistent reference for all practitioners.

The Architect of Self: The core tenet that each individual possesses the inherent power, responsibility, and agency to consciously choose their actions and shape their own path, character, and reality.

The Chronicle of Unveiling (The Chronicle): The foundational text of The Path of Unveiling. It is considered a living document, intended to be a guide for practitioners and to evolve with the collective wisdom of the community.

The Ethical Compass: The set of moral principles that guides action on The Path, founded on the dual pillars of **Compassion** and **Reason**. Its principles include Striving for Justice, Bodily Autonomy, and Reasoned Error Correction.

The Five Laws of Existence: A set of metaphorical principles that describe the fundamental nature of reality. They are: 1. You Exist; 2. Everything is Here and Now; 3. The One is The All, and The All is The One; 4. What You Put Out is What You Get Back; 5. Everything Changes (Except for the First Four Laws).

Gnosis: Direct, experiential knowing or inner wisdom that blossoms from within through introspection, intuition, and direct engagement with reality, rather than from external dogma or authority.

The Global Hearth: The envisioned future state of humanity characterized by universal interconnectedness, collective harmony, and a shared commitment to the well-being of all life on the planet.

The Grand Tapestry: The foundational tenet that all existence—from atoms to galaxies, thoughts to actions—is fundamentally interconnected in a single, magnificent, and evolving system.

The Guiding Hand: The archetype for the transmission of wisdom on The Path, embodied by experienced practitioners who mentor and support others on their journey.

Hearth (or Unveiling Hearth): A sanctuary and community of practice where individuals gather to explore, practice, and embody the principles of The Path in a supportive, non-dogmatic environment.

The Inner Compass: The innate faculty of inner wisdom, intuition, and discernment that guides an individual's journey. Cultivating and listening to this compass is a central practice of The Path.

Keeper: An experienced practitioner who takes on the role of nurturing and facilitating a local Unveiling Hearth, serving as a guide and steward for the community.

The Living Chronicle: The dynamic, ever-unfolding record of all existence, encompassing every personal narrative and collective story. Practitioners contribute to it through their lived experiences.

The Living Vessel: The wisdom of the body and the senses. It recognizes the body not as a mere container, but as an intelligent system and a sacred instrument of Gnosis.

The Luminous Spark: The intrinsic, vital energy of play, humor, and joy, seen as an essential wellspring of vitality, creativity, and resilience on The Path.

The Path of Unveiling (The Path): A secular journey of discovery and a framework for personal growth, ethical living, and deep connection, guided by inner wisdom and universal principles synthesized from humanity's collective heritage.

The Perpetual Becoming: The tenet that all of existence, including the self, is in a continuous and ceaseless process of transformation, adaptation, growth, and evolution.

The Resonant Echo: The tenet recognizing the profound power of story, myth, symbol, and archetype to convey universal truths and shape human experience across cultures and generations.

The River of Now: The profound practice of presence and mindfulness, recognizing that all of reality unfolds in the present moment, which is the only true point of creation and experience.

The Scales of Being: The tenet that true flourishing arises from a dynamic balance and harmony between complementary forces (e.g., light and shadow, action and rest), recognized as a continuous process of integration and adjustment.

The Symphony of Self: The harmonious integration of all aspects of one's being—physical, emotional, mental, and spiritual—into a coherent, authentic, and evolving whole.

Unveiler: A highly experienced and deeply integrated practitioner who provides personalized mentorship and deeper guidance to individuals or small groups on The Path.

Walker: An individual actively engaged in their personal journey on The Path, seeking to deepen their understanding and practice, often with the support of a Hearth or mentor.

Wanderer: An individual who is new to or exploring The Path, often bringing diverse perspectives from other traditions before choosing to engage more deeply.

The Weave of Repair: A conscious process for navigating conflict, practicing forgiveness, and striving for reconciliation by applying the principles of *The Ethical Compass* to restore harmony within relationships.

The Wellspring Within: The inner reservoir of physical, emotional, and mental energy that is nurtured through sustainable practice and conscious self-care, recognized as essential for an enduring journey.

Addenda

Addendum I: The Cosmic Tapestry – Our Starseed Origins and the Grand Volunteer Program

*The human story, as told by conventional history, often begins with our emergence on this planet, a singular event in a vast, indifferent cosmos. Yet, ancient whispers and modern intuitions suggest a grander narrative—one that stretches beyond Earth's confines, connecting our origins to the very stars. On **The Path of Unveiling**, we explore the concept of "Starseed Origins" and a "Grand Volunteer Program" not as literal, verifiable history, but as a profound **Symbolic Language (Chapter XVII)** and a powerful **Personal Narrative (Addendum XIX)** that can deepen our understanding of **The Grand Tapestry (Chapter I)**, inspire our **Perpetual Becoming (Chapter IV)**, and illuminate our sense of purpose.*

*This addendum offers a framework for understanding these concepts through a secular, metaphorical lens, recognizing their capacity to foster a sense of cosmic belonging, universal interconnectedness, and a profound **Responsibility and Agency (Chapter V)** in shaping our collective future. It is a story that resonates with **The Resonant Echo (Chapter VI)**, speaking to a deep, archetypal yearning for connection beyond the familiar.*

I. Defining Starseed Origins and the Grand Volunteer Program on The Path

Within The Path of Unveiling, these concepts are understood as:

- **Starseed Origins (Metaphorical):** The idea that some individuals feel a deep, inexplicable connection to distant star systems or a sense of not fully belonging to Earth. Metaphorically, this represents a profound intuition of **cosmic interconnectedness (The Grand Tapestry - Chapter I)** and a recognition that the very elements of our bodies were forged in stars (**Chapter XIV. Scientific Insights**). It speaks to a soul-level yearning for a broader cosmic awareness and a sense of a larger purpose that transcends immediate earthly concerns.

- **Grand Volunteer Program (Archetypal Narrative):** The concept that certain souls "volunteered" to incarnate on Earth during pivotal times to assist in humanity's evolution, particularly in raising consciousness and fostering a more harmonious existence. Archetypally, this represents a deep, innate drive for **service, compassion, and positive change**. It is a powerful **Personal Narrative (Addendum XIX)** that can empower individuals to embrace their **Responsibility and Agency (Chapter V)** in contributing to the well-being of **The Grand Tapestry (Chapter I)**.

II. The Cosmic Tapestry and The Core Tenets of The Path

1. **The Grand Tapestry:** The very name of this concept reflects its profound connection to **The Interconnectedness of All Being (Chapter I)**. It expands our understanding of this tapestry to a cosmic scale, suggesting that humanity is not isolated but an integral part of a vast, intelligent, and interconnected universe. It fosters **The Cosmic Reverence (Addendum XIV)**.

2. **The Inner Compass:** For individuals who resonate with these concepts, the feeling of "Starseed Origins" often serves as a powerful intuitive signal, a deep inner knowing that guides their life choices and sense of purpose. It is a form of **Gnosis (Chapter II)** that speaks to a profound, non-cognitive understanding of their place in the universe.

3. **The Perpetual Becoming:** The narrative of a "Grand Volunteer Program" inherently implies a commitment to **Transformation and Growth (Chapter IV)**, both personal and collective. It suggests an ongoing process of evolution, where individuals contribute to the raising of planetary consciousness, aligning with **The Ethical Compass (Chapter XI)**.

4. **The Architect of Self:** Embracing the narrative of a "volunteer" empowers individuals to step into their **Responsibility and Agency (Chapter V)**. It provides a compelling story for why one might feel driven to contribute to positive change, fostering a proactive

approach to shaping one's life and impact. It is a powerful **Personal Narrative (Addendum XIX)**.

5. **The Resonant Echo:** The idea of cosmic origins and benevolent guidance resonates with ancient myths of "sky people," divine interventions, and universal archetypes of service and destiny. It taps into a deep, collective human yearning for meaning and connection beyond the earthly realm, finding echoes in **Mythological Archetypes (Chapter XII)**.

III. Practices for Embodiment: Weaving Your Cosmic Thread

1. **Cosmic Meditation/Visualization:**
    - **Practice:** Find a quiet space. Close your eyes and visualize yourself floating in the vastness of space. See Earth as a beautiful blue marble, and then expand your awareness to include the solar system, the galaxy, and the entire universe. Feel your physical body as a tiny, yet vital, part of this immense **Grand Tapestry (Chapter I)**. Reflect on the stardust within you (**Chapter XIV. Scientific Insights**).
    - **Purpose:** To cultivate a profound sense of **Cosmic Reverence (Addendum XIV)**, interconnectedness, and humility in the face of the universe's scale. This can help quiet the ego and deepen **The Inner Compass (Chapter II)**.

2. **"Cosmic Purpose" Journaling:**
   - **Practice:** Reflect on moments in your life where you felt a strong, inexplicable pull towards a particular cause, a sense of deep empathy for humanity, or a profound desire to contribute to something larger than yourself. Journal about these feelings. If the "Starseed" narrative resonates, explore what qualities or "missions" you feel called to embody.
   - **Purpose:** To clarify your **Responsibility and Agency (Chapter V)** and consciously align your actions with a felt sense of purpose, contributing to your **Personal Narrative (Addendum XIX)**.

3. **Connection to Universal Archetypes:**
   - **Practice:** Explore **Mythological Archetypes (Chapter XII)** or **Symbolic Language (Chapter XVII)** (e.g., Tarot, Astrology) that speak to themes of cosmic connection, wisdom, or service. Reflect on how these symbols resonate with your inner experience of "Starseed" qualities.
   - **Purpose:** To provide a language and framework for understanding intuitive feelings and to connect personal experience to broader, universal patterns, deepening **The Resonant Echo (Chapter VI)**.

4. **Embodied Service:**
   - **Practice:** Translate any felt sense of "volunteer mission" into tangible action. This could involve

environmental stewardship (**The Ethical Footprint - Addendum XVI**), advocating for social justice (**Striving for Justice - Chapter XI**), fostering community harmony (**The Weave of Repair - Addendum XIII**), or simply embodying **Compassion and Reason (Chapter XI)** in your daily interactions.
- o **Purpose:** To ground the metaphorical narrative in concrete, ethical action, manifesting **The Architect of Self (Chapter V)**.

5. **Honoring the "Other":**
    - o **Practice:** Reflect on how the concept of "extraterrestrial kinship" (as explored in **Addendum III: The Path of Light**) can expand your capacity for **Compassion (Chapter XI)** and understanding towards all beings, even those who seem vastly different from yourself.
    - o **Purpose:** To dissolve perceived barriers of separation and reinforce the fundamental unity of **The Grand Tapestry (Chapter I)**.

By engaging with **The Cosmic Tapestry** as a powerful metaphorical framework, practitioners of The Path of Unveiling can unlock a deeper sense of cosmic belonging, inspire their **Perpetual Becoming (Chapter IV)**, and empower their **Responsibility and Agency (Chapter V)** in contributing to the flourishing of all life within **The Grand Tapestry (Chapter I)**.

Addendum II: The Subconscious Oracle – Accessing Inner Wisdom and Parallel Realities

Beyond the conscious mind, with its logical deductions and linear processing, lies a vast, often unseen realm of intuition, instinct, and profound insight. This is the domain of the subconscious—a powerful reservoir of information, memory, and creative potential that continuously influences our thoughts, feelings, and actions. On **The Path of Unveiling**, *we recognize the subconscious not as a mysterious, uncontrollable force, but as* **The Subconscious Oracle**—*an innate source of wisdom and a gateway to deeper understanding.*

This addendum explores how to consciously access and interpret the messages from this inner realm, reframing concepts like "parallel realities" as metaphorical expressions of our mind's capacity for diverse perspectives and potential outcomes. It is a vital practice for sharpening **The Inner Compass (Chapter II)**, *strengthening* **The Architect of Self (Chapter V)**, *and navigating our* **Perpetual Becoming (Chapter IV)** *with greater clarity and intuition.*

I. Defining The Subconscious Oracle and Parallel Realities on The Path

Within The Path of Unveiling, these concepts are understood as:

- **The Subconscious Oracle:** The non-conscious part of the mind that processes vast amounts of information, stores memories, regulates bodily functions, and influences our conscious thoughts and behaviors. It communicates through intuition, dreams, symbols, and subtle bodily sensations. It is a direct pathway to **Gnosis (Chapter II)** that bypasses purely rational thought.

- **Parallel Realities (Metaphorical):** The concept that multiple versions of reality or outcomes exist simultaneously. Metaphorically, this represents the mind's capacity to conceive of **alternative possibilities, perspectives, and potential futures.** It highlights the power of our perception and choices in shaping our experience, reinforcing our **Responsibility and Agency (Chapter V).** It is not about literal alternate dimensions, but about the vast spectrum of what *could be* or *could have been* within our experience.

II. The Subconscious Oracle and The Core Tenets of The Path

1. **The Inner Compass:** The Subconscious Oracle is a primary conduit for **Gnosis (Chapter II)** and the intuitive guidance of **The Inner Compass.** By learning to listen to its whispers (dreams, gut feelings), we access a deeper, non-linear form of wisdom that complements rational thought.

2. **The Architect of Self:** Understanding the subconscious empowers **The Architect of Self (Chapter V)**. By becoming aware of subconscious patterns, beliefs, and biases, we gain greater **Responsibility and Agency (Chapter V)** in consciously reshaping them to align with our intentions and values. This is crucial for intentional creation, as discussed in **Law 4: What You Put Out is What You Get Back (Addendum VII)**.

3. **The Perpetual Becoming:** Engaging with the subconscious facilitates **Transformation and Growth (Chapter IV)**. It allows us to identify and release limiting beliefs or past traumas that impede our progress, clearing the way for new patterns of thought and behavior. This process of release and integration aligns with **The Weave of Repair (Addendum XIII)** and **The Great Cycle (Addendum IX)**.

4. **The Resonant Echo:** The subconscious often communicates through **Symbolic Language (Chapter XVII)**, archetypes (**Chapter XII. Mythological Archetypes**), and metaphors found in myths and dreams. Learning to interpret these universal symbols helps us understand our inner world and connect to the collective human experience.

5. **The Living Vessel:** Our subconscious mind is deeply intertwined with our physical body. Sensations, "gut feelings," and psychosomatic responses are direct

communications from the subconscious, emphasizing the wisdom of **The Living Vessel (Addendum XII)** and the importance of interoceptive awareness.

III. Practices for Embodiment: Listening to the Oracle

1. **Dream Journaling and Interpretation:**
    - **Practice:** Keep a notebook and pen by your bed. Immediately upon waking, record any dreams, images, feelings, or thoughts, no matter how fragmented. Don't try to "figure it out" immediately; just capture it. Later, reflect on recurring symbols, emotions, or themes. How might they relate to your waking life, challenges, or aspirations?
    - **Purpose:** Dreams are a direct language of **The Subconscious Oracle**, offering insights, processing emotions, and sometimes providing creative solutions. This practice deepens **The Inner Compass (Chapter II)** and contributes to **The Living Chronicle (Addendum XIX)**.

2. **Intuitive Inquiry / "Gut Feeling" Awareness:**
    - **Practice:** Before making a decision or engaging in a new situation, pause. Tune into your **Living Vessel (Addendum XII)**. Notice any subtle physical sensations, emotional shifts, or spontaneous "knowings" that arise. Do you feel an expansive "yes" or a contracting "no"?

- **Purpose:** To develop sensitivity to your innate intuition, a rapid form of **Gnosis (Chapter II)** that often precedes conscious thought. This helps in making choices aligned with your deepest self, reinforcing **The Architect of Self (Chapter V)**.

3. **Active Imagination / Guided Visualization:**
    - **Practice:** In a relaxed state, hold a question or challenge in your mind. Allow images, symbols, or scenarios to spontaneously arise from your imagination. Engage with them as if they are real, asking them questions, observing their responses. This can be done through guided meditations or simply by allowing your mind to wander with intention.
    - **Purpose:** To consciously engage with the subconscious, allowing it to offer creative solutions, process emotions, or reveal hidden perspectives. This is a direct application of **The Power of Story and Symbol (Chapter VI)** and **Symbolic Language (Chapter XVII)**.

4. **Affirmation and Visualization for Manifestation:**
    - **Practice:** Once you've clarified an intention or desired outcome, create positive affirmations (e.g., "I am capable and resilient"). Visualize yourself already experiencing the desired reality, engaging all your senses. Repeat these affirmations and visualizations consistently.

- **Purpose:** To impress positive beliefs and intentions upon the subconscious, aligning its vast power with your conscious goals. This is a key aspect of **Responsibility and Agency (Chapter V)** and **Law 4: What You Put Out is What You Get Back (Addendum VII)**.

5. Shadow Work (Integration):
    - **Practice:** Consciously explore aspects of yourself that you have repressed or deemed "negative" (**The Shadow Archetype - Chapter XII**). This can be done through journaling, creative expression, or guided reflection. The goal is not to eliminate these parts, but to acknowledge, understand, and integrate them, finding their potential wisdom or energy.
    - **Purpose:** To achieve greater psychological wholeness and **Balance and Harmony (Chapter III)**, releasing internal conflict and freeing up energy for **Perpetual Becoming (Chapter IV)**. This is also crucial for **The Sacred Flame of Being (Addendum VIII)**.

By consciously engaging with **The Subconscious Oracle**, practitioners of The Path of Unveiling unlock a deeper, richer source of wisdom and creative power. They learn to navigate their inner landscapes with greater skill, transforming hidden patterns into conscious allies, and thereby empowering their **Architect of Self (Chapter V)** to shape a more intentional and fulfilling **Perpetual Becoming (Chapter IV)** within **The Grand Tapestry (Chapter I)**.

Addendum III: The Path of Light – Conscious Connection and Extraterrestrial Kinship

For millennia, humanity has gazed at the stars, wondering if we are alone in the vast cosmic ocean. This ancient curiosity has given rise to countless myths, legends, and increasingly, scientific inquiry. On **The Path of Unveiling***, we approach the concept of "Extraterrestrial Kinship" not as a matter of uncritical belief, but as a powerful* **Symbolic Language (Chapter XVII)** *and a profound* **Personal Narrative (Addendum XIX)** *that can expand our understanding of* **The Grand Tapestry (Chapter I)***, foster universal* **Compassion and Reason (Chapter XI)***, and inspire our collective* **Perpetual Becoming (Chapter IV)***.*

This addendum explores **The Path of Light**—*a metaphorical framework for cultivating conscious connection, both within ourselves and with the broader cosmos. It encourages an open-minded yet discerning approach to the idea of non-human intelligence, recognizing its capacity to deepen our sense of* **Cosmic Reverence (Addendum XIV)** *and reinforce our* **Responsibility and Agency (Chapter V)** *in shaping a harmonious future for all beings.*

I. Defining Conscious Connection and Extraterrestrial Kinship on The Path

Within The Path of Unveiling, these concepts are understood as:

- **Conscious Connection:** The intentional cultivation of heightened awareness and empathy, extending beyond immediate human relationships to encompass all life on Earth and, metaphorically, to potential intelligent life beyond our planet. It is a practice of expanding **The Inner Compass (Chapter II)** to perceive deeper levels of interconnectedness.

- **Extraterrestrial Kinship (Metaphorical/Archetypal):** The concept that humanity may share a fundamental connection or "kinship" with intelligent life forms from other parts of the cosmos. Metaphorically, this represents a profound intuition of **universal interconnectedness (The Grand Tapestry - Chapter I)** and a recognition that life, in its myriad forms, is a pervasive phenomenon. Archetypally, it speaks to our collective yearning for belonging and a broader cosmic family, resonating with **Mythological Archetypes (Chapter XII)** of "sky people" or benevolent guides. It can also be seen as an extension of **Addendum I: The Cosmic Tapestry**, which explores our "Starseed Origins."

II. The Path of Light and The Core Tenets of The Path

1. **The Grand Tapestry:** The idea of extraterrestrial kinship profoundly expands our understanding of **The Interconnectedness of All Being (Chapter I)**. It suggests

that the tapestry of life extends far beyond Earth, fostering a sense of belonging to a cosmic whole and deepening **The Cosmic Reverence (Addendum XIV)**.

2. **The Inner Compass:** Engaging with the concept of extraterrestrial kinship, even metaphorically, can stimulate **The Inner Compass (Chapter II)**, encouraging open-mindedness, intuitive exploration, and a willingness to consider possibilities beyond conventional understanding. It can be a powerful source of **Gnosis.**

3. **The Ethical Compass:** The concept of universal kinship inherently promotes **Compassion and Reason (Chapter XI)** towards all forms of life, regardless of origin. It challenges anthropocentric biases and encourages a broader ethical framework that encompasses potential non-human intelligences. This aligns with **Striving for Justice (Chapter XI)** for all beings.

4. **The Perpetual Becoming:** The notion of humanity evolving towards "conscious connection" with extraterrestrial life suggests a profound collective **Transformation and Growth (Chapter IV)**. It implies a future where humanity transcends its current limitations and integrates into a larger cosmic community.

5. **The Resonant Echo:** The idea of contact with benevolent "others" resonates deeply with ancient myths and prophecies across cultures, reflecting a universal human

longing for guidance, wisdom, and connection beyond the earthly realm. This is explored in **Chapter XII. Mythological Archetypes** and **Chapter XVII. Symbolic Language**.

6. **The Architect of Self:** Embracing the possibility of extraterrestrial kinship can empower individuals to feel a greater sense of **Responsibility and Agency (Chapter V)** in preparing humanity for a broader cosmic awareness, fostering a proactive approach to global harmony and conscious evolution.

III. Practices for Embodiment: Illuminating the Path of Light

1. **Cosmic Contemplation & Openness:**
   - **Practice:** Spend time under the night sky, consciously contemplating the vastness of the universe and the potential for life beyond Earth. Practice an open-minded stance, allowing for the possibility of diverse forms of intelligence without judgment or fear. This deepens **The Cosmic Reverence (Addendum XIV)**.
   - **Purpose:** To expand your perception of **The Grand Tapestry (Chapter I)** and cultivate a sense of awe, humility, and curiosity towards the unknown, aligning with **The Wisdom of Humility (Addendum XV)**.

2. **Universal Compassion Meditation:**

- **Practice:** Engage in a meditation practice where you extend feelings of **Compassion (Chapter XI)** and goodwill not just to humans, but to all sentient beings on Earth, and then beyond, to all potential life forms in the cosmos. Visualize a network of light connecting all consciousness.
- **Purpose:** To cultivate a profound sense of universal kinship and to dissolve perceived barriers of separation, reinforcing **The Grand Tapestry (Chapter I)**.

3. **"First Contact" Scenario Reflection:**
    - **Practice:** Engage in thought experiments or journaling about how humanity might ethically and wisely approach a hypothetical "first contact" scenario. What values would you want humanity to embody? How would you ensure **Respect for Others' Freedoms (Chapter XI)**?
    - **Purpose:** To prepare the mind for expanded consciousness, to proactively engage with ethical dilemmas, and to reinforce **Reason and Compassion (Chapter XI)** as guiding principles for future interactions. This is an exercise in **The Architect of Self (Chapter V)**.

4. Symbolic Communication & Intuitive Listening:
    - **Practice:** Explore **Symbolic Language (Chapter XVII)** systems like Tarot or Runes, or engage in **Dream Journaling (Addendum II: The**

Subconscious Oracle), with an intention to receive insights about universal connection or your role in the larger cosmic narrative. View these as communications from your subconscious or the collective unconscious, not literal messages from ETs.
   - **Purpose:** To access deeper intuitive wisdom (**The Inner Compass - Chapter II**) and to interpret archetypal messages that resonate with the theme of cosmic kinship, reinforcing **The Resonant Echo (Chapter VI)**.

5. **Embodied Universal Citizenship:**
   - **Practice:** Live your daily life as if you are a "citizen of the cosmos." How would this perspective influence your actions regarding environmental stewardship (**The Ethical Footprint - Addendum XVI**), global cooperation, and the pursuit of peace (**Striving for Justice - Chapter XI**)?
   - **Purpose:** To ground the metaphorical concept in tangible, ethical action, manifesting **Responsibility and Agency (Chapter V)** and contributing to the collective **Perpetual Becoming (Chapter IV)** of humanity.

By consciously walking **The Path of Light**, practitioners of The Path of Unveiling expand their sense of identity beyond earthly confines. They cultivate universal **Compassion and Reason (Chapter XI)**, deepen their **Cosmic Reverence**

(**Addendum XIV**), and proactively engage in their **Responsibility and Agency (Chapter V)** to foster a future of greater interconnectedness and harmony within **The Grand Tapestry (Chapter I)**.

Addendum IV: The Unveiling Hearth – *A Sanctuary for Cosmic Connection*

*While **The Path of Unveiling** is fundamentally a personal journey of **Gnosis** and **Perpetual Becoming (Chapter IV)**, it is not meant to be walked in isolation. Humanity thrives in community, finding strength, support, and shared meaning in collective endeavor. **The Unveiling Hearth** is the primary communal expression of The Path—a sanctuary where individuals gather to explore, practice, and embody its principles in a supportive, non-dogmatic environment.*

*This addendum outlines the vision and function of the Hearth, emphasizing its role in fostering **The Grand Tapestry (Chapter I)** of human connection, supporting individual **Architects of Self (Chapter V)**, and providing a space for collective **unveiling** and growth. It is a living embodiment of **The Ethical Compass (Chapter XI)**, built on principles of **Compassion and Reason**.*

I. Defining The Unveiling Hearth

Within The Path of Unveiling, **The Unveiling Hearth** is understood as:

- **A Sanctuary:** A safe, inclusive, and welcoming space (physical or virtual) where individuals can explore profound questions, engage in practices, and share their authentic selves without judgment.

- **A Community of Practice:** A group of individuals committed to walking **The Path of Unveiling**, supporting each other's journeys, and collectively embodying its principles. It is a micro-expression of **The Grand Tapestry (Chapter I)**.

- **A Crucible for Growth:** A dynamic environment that encourages **Transformation and Growth (Chapter IV)**, fosters **Reasoned Error Correction (Chapter XI)**, and provides a container for navigating challenges through **The Weave of Repair (Addendum XIII)**.

II. The Hearth and The Core Tenets of The Path

1. **The Grand Tapestry:** The Hearth is the foundational unit where the threads of individual lives are consciously woven into a stronger, more resilient collective fabric. It demonstrates the profound interconnectedness of human experience and fosters a sense of belonging.

2. **The Ethical Compass:** Hearths operate under the explicit guidance of **The Ethical Compass (Chapter XI)**, prioritizing **Compassion and Reason, Respect for Others' Freedoms**, and **Striving for Justice** within their interactions. Conflict resolution within the Hearth is guided by **The Weave of Repair (Addendum XIII)**.

3. **The Architect of Self:** While providing support, the Hearth empowers each individual to be their own **Architect of Self (Chapter V)**. It offers tools and a supportive environment for personal **Responsibility and Agency (Chapter V)**, rather than dictating beliefs or actions.

4. **The Inner Compass:** The Hearth provides a safe space for individuals to explore and share insights from their **Inner Compass (Chapter II)**, fostering a collective pursuit of **Gnosis** through shared reflection and dialogue.

5. **The Resonant Echo:** Hearths become living repositories of **The Resonant Echo (Chapter VI)**, where personal narratives (**The Living Chronicle - Addendum XIX**) are shared, collective wisdom is accumulated, and new stories of **unveiling** emerge.

6. **The Perpetual Becoming:** The Hearth supports the continuous **Transformation and Growth (Chapter IV)** of its members, providing a stable yet dynamic environment for learning, adaptation, and evolution.

III. Principles of Hearth Operation

1. **Inclusivity and Openness:** Hearths welcome all sincere seekers, regardless of background, identity, or prior beliefs. They are spaces of exploration, not exclusion. This aligns with **Respect for Others' Freedoms (Chapter XI)**.

2. **Non-Dogmatic Inquiry:** While guided by the principles of The Path, Hearths encourage critical thinking, open questioning, and personal discernment. There are no mandatory beliefs, only shared principles and practices. This embodies **The Wisdom of Humility (Addendum XV)**.

3. **Mutual Respect and Support:** Members commit to treating each other with dignity, empathy, and active support. Confidentiality and trust are paramount. This is a direct application of **Compassion and Reason (Chapter XI)**.

4. **Shared Responsibility:** Hearths are self-organizing to a degree, with members taking collective **Responsibility and Agency (Chapter V)** for their functioning, activities, and well-being.

5. **Focus on Practice and Experience:** While discussion is important, Hearths prioritize the embodiment of The Path's principles through shared practices, rituals, and

communal engagement, as outlined in **Part 2: Living the Path**.

IV. Activities and Functions of a Hearth

1. **Regular Gatherings:**
   - **Weekly/Bi-Weekly Sessions:** Focused on exploring specific tenets, engaging in practices (**Chapter VII. Daily Practices, Chapter VIII. Weekly & Monthly Cycles**), and sharing personal insights.
   - **Seasonal Observances:** Communal celebrations of the equinoxes and solstices (**Chapter IX. Seasonal Observances**), fostering connection to natural rhythms.

2. **Learning and Mentorship:**
   - **Guided Discussions:** Facilitated by **Keepers** or **Unveilers** (**Addendum XVII: The Guiding Hand**), exploring chapters of The Chronicle or specific addenda.
   - **Skill Sharing:** Members share practical skills relevant to mindful living, sustainability (**The Ethical Footprint - Addendum XVI**), or personal growth.
   - **Mentorship Opportunities:** Informal and formal mentorship between more experienced members (**Keepers/Unveilers**) and those newer to The Path (**Walkers/Wanderers**), as detailed in **Addendum XVII: The Guiding Hand**.

3. **Community Building:**
   - **Social Gatherings:** Informal events to foster camaraderie and deepen personal bonds, nurturing **The Luminous Spark (Addendum XI)**.
   - **Support Circles:** Spaces for members to share challenges and offer mutual support, applying principles from **The Weave of Repair (Addendum XIII)**.
   - **Shared Projects:** Collaborative initiatives that benefit the Hearth or the wider community, embodying **Striving for Justice (Chapter XI)** and **Conscious Consumption and Stewardship (Addendum XVI)**.

4. **Rites of Passage:**
   - Hearths facilitate and witness **Life Transitions (Chapter X)**, providing communal recognition and support for members navigating significant life events.

V. The Role of Keepers of the Hearth

- **Keepers** are dedicated practitioners who take on the **Responsibility and Agency (Chapter V)** of nurturing and facilitating the Hearth. They are not gurus or authorities, but guides and facilitators.

- **Responsibilities:** Organizing gatherings, facilitating discussions, ensuring adherence to **The Ethical Compass (Chapter XI)**, mediating conflicts (**The Weave of Repair - Addendum XIII**), and serving as a point of contact for new members. Their role is further detailed in **Addendum VI: The Council of Unveilers** and **Addendum XVII: The Guiding Hand.**

- **Self-Care:** Keepers are encouraged to prioritize their own **Wellspring Within (Addendum XVIII)** to sustain their service.

The Unveiling Hearth is more than just a meeting place; it is a dynamic, living ecosystem where individuals come together to deepen their **unveilings**, support each other's journeys, and collectively weave a more conscious and compassionate **Grand Tapestry (Chapter I)** for themselves and the world. It is a sanctuary for **Perpetual Becoming (Chapter IV)**, built on the enduring power of human connection.

Addendum V: The Living Path – The Principles of Evolution, Expression, and Engagement

*The Path of Unveiling is not a static doctrine, but a dynamic, evolving journey. Just as the universe itself is in constant motion (**The Perpetual Becoming - Chapter IV**), so too is our understanding of reality, our practices, and our collective wisdom. This addendum explores **The Living Path**—the inherent capacity of The Path of Unveiling to adapt, grow, express itself in diverse forms, and engage with the ever-changing world.*

*It emphasizes that authenticity on The Path means embracing continuous **Transformation and Growth (Chapter IV)**, finding creative ways to express its principles, and actively engaging with the challenges and opportunities of the present moment. This ensures that The Path remains relevant, vibrant, and a powerful force for positive change within **The Grand Tapestry (Chapter I)**.*

I. Defining The Living Path

Within The Path of Unveiling, **The Living Path** is understood as:

- **Dynamic and Adaptive:** It is not fixed in time or dogma. It evolves with new scientific understanding (**Chapter XIV. Scientific Insights**), philosophical insights (**Chapter

XIII. Philosophical Excerpts), and the collective wisdom gained from the experiences of its practitioners. This embodies **The Wisdom of Humility (Addendum XV)** and **Reasoned Error Correction (Chapter XI)**.

- **Expressed in Myriad Forms:** Its principles can be expressed through diverse personal practices, artistic endeavors, community initiatives, and forms of engagement, reflecting **The Resonant Echo (Chapter VI)** and **The Living Chronicle (Addendum XIX)**.

- **Engaged with the World:** It is not an insular or escapist philosophy. It actively encourages ethical engagement with societal challenges, environmental concerns, and the pursuit of human flourishing within **The Grand Tapestry (Chapter I)**.

II. The Living Path and The Core Tenets of The Path

1. **The Perpetual Becoming:** This addendum is a direct articulation of **Transformation and Growth (Chapter IV)** as a core principle. It emphasizes that The Path itself is continuously evolving, adapting, and refining its understanding and practices.

2. **The Architect of Self:** Each individual's unique **unveiling** contributes to the evolution of The Path. Practitioners are encouraged to apply their **Responsibility and Agency**

(**Chapter V**) to innovate, express, and embody the principles in ways that resonate authentically with them.

3. **The Grand Tapestry:** The Living Path thrives through the diverse contributions and expressions of its members, strengthening the collective fabric and ensuring its relevance to a wide array of human experiences. It acknowledges the interconnectedness of all elements within the Path's ecosystem.

4. **The Resonant Echo:** The Living Path encourages the creation of new **Resonant Echoes (Chapter VI)** through contemporary art, literature, and practices, while also re-interpreting and drawing inspiration from ancient wisdom in new ways.

5. **The Ethical Compass:** Active engagement with the world requires constant application of **The Ethical Compass (Chapter XI)**. The Living Path calls for its principles to be applied to emerging global challenges, fostering **Striving for Justice** and **Conscious Consumption and Stewardship (Addendum XVI)**.

6. **The Inner Compass:** The evolution of The Path is guided by the collective and individual **Inner Compass (Chapter II)** of its practitioners, ensuring that adaptations remain aligned with core principles and ethical discernment (**Gnosis**).

III. Practices for Embodiment: Nurturing The Living Path

1. **Continuous Learning and Open Inquiry:**
    - **Practice:** Actively seek new knowledge in science, philosophy, psychology, and other fields that expand your understanding of reality. Engage in respectful dialogue with those holding different perspectives. This embodies **Scientific Understanding (Chapter XI)** and **The Wisdom of Humility (Addendum XV)**.
    - **Purpose:** To ensure that The Path remains intellectually vibrant and responsive to new insights, fostering **Perpetual Becoming (Chapter IV)**.

2. **Creative Expression of Principles:**
    - **Practice:** Find personal ways to express the tenets of The Path through art, writing, music, dance, or other creative mediums. This could be writing a poem about **The Grand Tapestry (Chapter I)**, composing music inspired by **The Luminous Spark (Addendum XI)**, or creating visual art that represents **The Scales of Being (Chapter III)**.
    - **Purpose:** To deepen personal understanding, share insights in resonant ways, and contribute to the growing body of **The Resonant Echo (Chapter VI)** and **The Living Chronicle (Addendum XIX)**.

3. **Ethical Engagement and Action:**

- **Practice:** Identify areas in your community or the world where you can apply the principles of **The Ethical Compass (Chapter XI)**. This might involve advocating for environmental protection (**The Ethical Footprint - Addendum XVI**), supporting social justice initiatives (**Striving for Justice - Chapter XI**), or participating in **The Weave of Repair (Addendum XIII)** within your local community.
- **Purpose:** To ground The Path in tangible, positive impact, demonstrating **Responsibility and Agency (Chapter V)** and contributing to the flourishing of **The Grand Tapestry (Chapter I)**.

4. **Adaptation of Practices:**
   - **Practice:** Experiment with the practices outlined in **Part 2: Living the Path**. Adapt them to fit your unique circumstances, cultural background, and personal preferences, while remaining true to their underlying purpose. Share your successful adaptations within your Hearth.
   - **Purpose:** To ensure the practices remain relevant and effective for diverse individuals, fostering personal **Perpetual Becoming (Chapter IV)**.

5. **Cultivating a "Future-Oriented" Mindset:**
   - **Practice:** Regularly reflect on how current trends and emerging knowledge might influence the future of humanity and the planet. Consider how

The Path's principles can offer guidance for navigating these future challenges and opportunities. This connects to **The River of Now (Addendum X)** and **The Great Cycle (Addendum IX)**.

- **Purpose:** To maintain foresight and adaptability, ensuring The Path remains a relevant and proactive guide for conscious evolution.

By embracing **The Living Path**, practitioners of The Path of Unveiling become active co-creators of its evolution. They ensure that this profound journey remains vibrant, relevant, and a powerful force for personal **Transformation and Growth (Chapter IV)** and collective flourishing within **The Grand Tapestry (Chapter I)** of existence.

Addendum VI: The Council of Unveilers – *Guiding the Living Path*

*As **The Path of Unveiling** grows and expands, a need arises for collective stewardship—a body of experienced practitioners dedicated to upholding its core principles, ensuring its ethical integrity, and guiding its evolution. This addendum introduces **The Council of Unveilers**—a collective of highly experienced and deeply integrated individuals who serve as the philosophical and ethical stewards of The Path.*

*The Council is not a governing body in the traditional sense, but a collective of wisdom keepers committed to nurturing **The Living Path (Addendum V)**. Their role is to provide guidance, facilitate coherence, and ensure that The Path remains true to its non-dogmatic, humanistic, and evolving nature, always prioritizing **Compassion and Reason (Chapter XI)** within **The Grand Tapestry (Chapter I)**.*

I. Defining The Council of Unveilers

Within The Path of Unveiling, **The Council of Unveilers** is understood as:

- **A Collective of Wisdom Keepers:** Composed of individuals who have profoundly embodied the principles of The Path, achieved deep **Gnosis (Chapter II)**, and demonstrated exceptional **Responsibility and Agency (Chapter V)** in their lives and service.

- **Stewards of Principles:** Their primary function is to safeguard the philosophical integrity and ethical consistency of The Path, ensuring it remains aligned with its core tenets and does not drift into dogma or rigid orthodoxy. This aligns with **The Ethical Compass (Chapter XI)**.

- **Facilitators of Evolution:** They actively support **The Living Path (Addendum V)**, encouraging its adaptation, growth, and expression in response to new insights and the changing needs of humanity. This embodies **The Perpetual Becoming (Chapter IV)** and **The Wisdom of Humility (Addendum XV)**.

II. The Council's Role and The Core Tenets of The Path

1. **The Ethical Compass:** The Council's very existence is an embodiment of **The Ethical Compass (Chapter XI)**. They are responsible for upholding **Compassion and Reason**, ensuring **Striving for Justice**, and facilitating **Reasoned Error Correction** within the broader Path community.

2. **The Guiding Hand (Addendum XVII):** The Council plays a crucial role in the **Transmission of Wisdom**, both directly through their own insights and indirectly by

overseeing the certification of **Unveilers** and **Keepers** who serve as mentors and guides.

3. **The Grand Tapestry:** The Council acts as a unifying force, helping to weave together the diverse threads of individual Hearths and practitioners into a cohesive, interconnected global community. They foster a sense of shared purpose and belonging.

4. **The Architect of Self:** While guiding, the Council respects the **Responsibility and Agency (Chapter V)** of each individual practitioner. Their role is to empower, not to dictate, fostering self-authorship within the framework of shared principles.

5. **The Perpetual Becoming:** The Council's commitment to **The Living Path (Addendum V)** means they actively embrace **Transformation and Growth (Chapter IV)** for The Path itself, ensuring it remains relevant and dynamic.

6. **The Resonant Echo:** The Council helps to curate and preserve **The Living Chronicle (Addendum XIX)** of The Path, ensuring that the collective wisdom and **Personal Narratives** of its practitioners resonate forward through time.

III. Functions of The Council of Unveilers

1. **Philosophical and Ethical Stewardship:**
    - **Principle Interpretation:** Offer guidance on the interpretation and application of The Path's core tenets and **The Ethical Compass (Chapter XI)** in complex situations.
    - **Ethical Review:** Serve as a final ethical review board for significant disputes or challenges that cannot be resolved at the Hearth level (**The Weave of Repair - Addendum XIII**).
    - **Consistency:** Work to ensure a consistent philosophical and ethical foundation across all Hearths and materials associated with The Path.

2. **Guidance for The Living Path:**
    - **Evolutionary Oversight:** Facilitate discussions and initiatives that explore how The Path can adapt and grow in response to new scientific discoveries (**Chapter XIV. Scientific Insights**), societal changes, and collective insights.
    - **Resource Development:** Oversee the creation and dissemination of foundational resources and learning materials for practitioners and Hearths.
    - **Inter-Hearth Connection:** Foster communication and collaboration between different Unveiling Hearths globally, strengthening **The Grand Tapestry (Chapter I)**.

3. **Certification and Support:**

- **Unveiler and Keeper Certification:** Establish and oversee the process for certifying **Unveilers** and **Keepers**, ensuring they meet criteria for experience, wisdom, and embodiment of The Path's principles. This is crucial for **The Guiding Hand (Addendum XVII)**.
- **Support for Keepers:** Provide resources, training, and ongoing support for **Keepers of the Hearth (Addendum IV)**, helping them to sustain their **Wellspring Within (Addendum XVIII)** and effectively facilitate their communities.
- **Conflict Resolution Training:** Ensure that **Keepers** and **Unveilers** are trained in principles of **The Weave of Repair (Addendum XIII)** to effectively navigate conflict within their Hearths.

IV. Membership and Structure

- **Composition:** The Council is comprised of a limited number of highly experienced **Unveilers** chosen for their profound wisdom, ethical integrity, and demonstrated commitment to The Path.

- **Selection:** Members are typically nominated by existing Council members or by a consensus of **Unveilers** and **Keepers**, and then undergo a rigorous review process focusing on their embodiment of The Path's principles and their capacity for compassionate leadership.

- **Term Limits/Rotation:** To prevent stagnation and ensure fresh perspectives, Council membership operates on a rotating basis with defined terms.

- **Decision-Making:** Decisions are made through a process of consensus-building and reasoned dialogue, embodying **The Scales of Being (Chapter III)** and **Reasoned Error Correction (Chapter XI)**.

The Council of Unveilers serves as a vital anchor for **The Living Path (Addendum V)**, providing a collective **Guiding Hand (Addendum XVII)** that nurtures its growth, preserves its integrity, and ensures its continued flourishing as a beacon of **unveiling** for humanity within **The Grand Tapestry (Chapter I)**.

Addendum VII: The Five Laws of Existence – *A Cosmic Mirror for The Path*

*Throughout history, humanity has sought to understand the fundamental principles governing reality. While science explores the physical laws of the universe, and philosophy grapples with existential truths, some traditions propose overarching "laws" that resonate across all dimensions of being—physical, mental, and spiritual. On **The Path of Unveiling**, we explore **The Five Laws of Existence** not as dogmatic decrees, but as a powerful **Symbolic Language (Chapter XVII)** and a **Cosmic Mirror** that reflects the core tenets of our Path.*

*These laws, often channeled or intuited from various sources, offer a framework for understanding the inherent order of **The Grand Tapestry (Chapter I)** and for aligning our **Responsibility and Agency (Chapter V)** with the natural flow of existence. They are a profound **Resonant Echo (Chapter VI)**, providing a simplified yet powerful lens through which to deepen our **Inner Compass (Chapter II)** and accelerate our **Perpetual Becoming (Chapter IV)**.*

I. Defining The Five Laws of Existence on The Path

Within The Path of Unveiling, **The Five Laws of Existence** are understood as:

- **Metaphorical Principles:** They are not literal, empirically verifiable laws in the scientific sense, but rather archetypal truths that describe the fundamental nature of reality and consciousness.

- **Tools for Gnosis:** They serve as prompts for introspection and direct experiential understanding (**Gnosis - Chapter II**), helping individuals to intuitively grasp complex universal dynamics.

- **Guides for Action:** They offer practical guidance for living in harmony with the universe, informing our **Ethical Compass (Chapter XI)** and empowering our **Architect of Self (Chapter V)**.

II. The Five Laws of Existence and The Core Tenets of The Path

1. **The Grand Tapestry:** These laws describe the fundamental operating system of **The Interconnectedness of All Being (Chapter I)**, illustrating how everything is woven together.

2. **The Inner Compass:** Understanding and applying these laws sharpens **The Inner Compass (Chapter II)**, providing a framework for intuitive discernment and aligning with universal wisdom.

3. **The Scales of Being:** The laws often highlight the dynamic interplay of forces and the inherent balance within the universe, reinforcing **Balance and Harmony (Chapter III)**.

4. **The Perpetual Becoming:** They speak to the continuous **Transformation and Growth (Chapter IV)** inherent in all existence and in our personal journeys.

5. **The Architect of Self:** They empower individuals to take **Responsibility and Agency (Chapter V)** for their lives by understanding how their consciousness and actions shape their reality.

6. **The Resonant Echo:** These universal principles resonate with wisdom traditions across time and cultures, forming a deep **Resonant Echo (Chapter VI)**.

III. The Five Laws (As Understood on The Path)

Law 1: You Exist
- **Core Idea:** The fundamental truth of consciousness and being. Before anything else, there is existence.
- **Relevance to The Path:** This law is the bedrock of **The Living Vessel (Addendum XII)** and the starting point for all **Gnosis (Chapter II)**. It affirms the inherent reality of our consciousness and our place within **The Grand**

Tapestry (**Chapter I**). It encourages presence and appreciation for the simple fact of being.
- **Reflection:** How does the simple affirmation of your existence ground you in the present moment? What does it mean to truly "be"?

Law 2: Everything is Here and Now

- **Core Idea:** All of existence, all possibilities, and all time are fundamentally accessible in the present moment. The past and future are dimensions of the "eternal now."
- **Relevance to The Path:** This law directly aligns with **The River of Now (Addendum X)**, emphasizing the power and richness of the present moment. It encourages mindfulness and presence in daily practices (**Chapter VII. Daily Practices**) and helps individuals transcend anxieties about the past or future by focusing their **Responsibility and Agency (Chapter V)** on the current reality. It connects to the idea that all potential "parallel realities" are accessible in the present, as explored in **The Subconscious Oracle (Addendum II)**.
- **Reflection:** How can embracing the "here and now" deepen your experience of life and empower your choices in this moment?

Law 3: The One is The All, and The All is The One

- **Core Idea:** Everything is interconnected; the individual is a microcosm of the macrocosm. Unity underlies all apparent diversity.

- **Relevance to The Path:** This is a direct articulation of **The Interconnectedness of All Being (The Grand Tapestry - Chapter I)**. It emphasizes that separation is an illusion and that our individual essence is part of a greater whole. It fosters **The Cosmic Reverence (Addendum XIV)** and universal **Compassion (Chapter XI)**. This also connects to **Addendum I: The Cosmic Tapestry** and **Addendum III: The Path of Light** by expanding our sense of kinship.
- **Reflection:** How does recognizing your intrinsic connection to all things deepen your sense of belonging and responsibility within **The Grand Tapestry**?

Law 4: What You Put Out is What You Get Back
- **Core Idea:** The principle of cause and effect, or energetic resonance. Your thoughts, intentions, actions, and emotions create a vibrational output that attracts similar experiences back to you. This is often referred to as "karma" or "the law of attraction."
- **Relevance to The Path:** This law profoundly empowers **The Architect of Self (Chapter V)**. It highlights our **Responsibility and Agency (Chapter V)** in consciously shaping our reality through our internal and external output. It is a practical application of **The Ethical Compass (Chapter XI)**, as ethical actions and positive intentions tend to lead to beneficial outcomes. This is also a key principle for understanding the influence of **The Subconscious Oracle (Addendum II)** on manifestation and for **The Weave of Repair (Addendum XIII)**, emphasizing accountability and the impact of our actions.

- **Reflection:** How can you consciously align your thoughts, words, and actions with the reality you wish to create for yourself and others?

Law 5: Everything Changes (Except for the First Four Laws)
- **Core Idea:** Everything in the universe is in a perpetual state of flux, evolution, and transformation. The only constant within manifestation is change itself, while the fundamental principles (the first four laws) remain constant.
- **Relevance to The Path:** This is a direct articulation of **Transformation and Growth (The Perpetual Becoming - Chapter IV)**. It encourages adaptability, resilience, and an acceptance of life's inherent impermanence. It aligns with **The River of Now (Addendum X)** and **The Great Cycle (Addendum IX)**, which explore the cycles of life and death. It also supports **The Wisdom of Humility (Addendum XV)** by reminding us that all things are temporary, while the underlying universal mechanics endure. This law provides a stable framework for our **Inner Compass (Chapter II)** amidst the dynamic nature of reality, ensuring that while our understanding evolves (**The Living Path - Addendum V**), these core principles remain.
- **Reflection:** How can you embrace change as an opportunity for growth rather than a source of fear? Where in your life can you flow more with the current of **Perpetual Becoming**? How does the understanding of

these unchanging first four laws provide a sense of stability amidst the constant change?

By contemplating and integrating **The Five Laws of Existence**, practitioners of
The Path of Unveiling gain a deeper, intuitive understanding of the fundamental mechanics of reality. This metaphorical framework empowers their **Architect of Self (Chapter V)**, sharpens their **Inner Compass (Chapter II)**, and guides their **Perpetual Becoming (Chapter IV)** in harmony with **The Grand Tapestry (Chapter I)**.

Addendum VIII: The Sacred Flame of Being – *Sexuality on The Path*

Sexuality, in its broadest sense, is a fundamental aspect of the human experience—a powerful force of creation, connection, and self-expression. Yet, throughout history, it has often been shrouded in taboo, shame, or rigid dogma, leading to suppression, misunderstanding, and disconnection from its inherent wisdom. On **The Path of Unveiling***, we recognize sexuality as* **The Sacred Flame of Being***—an intrinsic, vital energy that, when approached with* **Compassion and Reason (Chapter XI)***, can be a profound source of* **Gnosis (Chapter II)***, personal growth, and deep connection within* **The Grand Tapestry (Chapter I)***.*

This addendum explores sexuality as a natural, healthy, and integral part of **The Living Vessel (Addendum XII)***. It emphasizes conscious engagement, ethical practice, and the cultivation of authentic intimacy, freeing this powerful energy from judgment and reclaiming it as a pathway to self-awareness, joy, and profound human connection. It is a vital aspect of* **The Architect of Self (Chapter V)***, shaping our most intimate expressions.*

I. Defining The Sacred Flame of Being on The Path
Within The Path of Unveiling, **The Sacred Flame of Being** is understood as:

- **Life Force Energy:** The inherent creative, generative, and connective energy present in all living beings. It manifests not only in procreation but also in passion, creativity, vitality, and the drive for connection.

- **A Pathway to Gnosis:** When approached mindfully, sexual energy can lead to heightened states of awareness, deep insight, and a profound sense of unity, offering a unique form of **Gnosis (Chapter II)**.

- **Integral to The Living Vessel:** Sexuality is a natural and healthy function of the human body, deeply intertwined with physical, emotional, and psychological well-being. This aligns with the wisdom of **The Living Vessel (Addendum XII)**.

- **An Expression of The Architect of Self:** Our sexual choices and expressions are powerful acts of **Responsibility and Agency (Chapter V)**, reflecting our values, boundaries, and desires.

II. The Sacred Flame of Being and The Core Tenets of The Path

1. **The Ethical Compass:** Sexuality is approached through the explicit framework of **The Ethical Compass (Chapter XI)**. Principles like **Bodily Autonomy, Respect for Others' Freedoms, Compassion and Reason**, and **Striving for Justice** are paramount, ensuring all sexual expression is

consensual, respectful, and free from harm. This includes enthusiastic consent in all interactions.

2. **The Living Vessel:** Sexuality is deeply rooted in the physical and energetic body. Honoring **The Sacred Flame** means listening to the wisdom of **The Living Vessel (Addendum XII)**, understanding its needs, and respecting its boundaries.

3. **The Scales of Being:** Healthy sexuality involves **Balance and Harmony (Chapter III)** between giving and receiving, passion and tenderness, individual desire and relational needs. It also involves integrating aspects of self often pushed into the "shadow" (**The Shadow Archetype - Chapter XII**) due to societal conditioning or shame.

4. **The Architect of Self:** Conscious sexual expression is a powerful act of **Responsibility and Agency (Chapter V)**. It involves self-awareness, clear communication, and the intentional shaping of one's sexual narrative and experiences, contributing to **The Living Chronicle (Addendum XIX)**.

5. **The Grand Tapestry:** Sexual connection, in its broadest sense, is a fundamental aspect of human connection, contributing to the intricate weave of **The Grand Tapestry (Chapter I)** through intimacy, family, and community bonds.

6. **The Luminous Spark:** When expressed authentically and ethically, sexuality can be a profound source of joy, pleasure, and vitality, igniting **The Luminous Spark (Addendum XI)** within individuals and relationships.

7. **The Perpetual Becoming:** Our understanding and expression of sexuality evolve throughout life. It is a journey of continuous **Transformation and Growth (Chapter IV)**, requiring openness, learning, and adaptation. This includes embracing the **Sacred Feminine** and masculine energies as part of our **Perpetual Becoming**.

III. Principles for Conscious Sexual Engagement

1. **Enthusiastic Consent (The Foundation of Respect):**
    - **Principle:** All sexual activity must be predicated on clear, enthusiastic, ongoing, and freely given consent from all parties involved. Silence or absence of "no" is not consent.
    - **Application:** Practice clear communication about desires, boundaries, and comfort levels. Understand that consent can be withdrawn at any time. This is a direct application of **Bodily Autonomy (Chapter XI)** and **Respect for Others' Freedoms (Chapter XI)**.

2. **Self-Awareness (The Inner Compass):**

- **Principle:** Understand your own desires, boundaries, and emotional landscape related to sexuality. Recognize the influence of past experiences, societal conditioning, and subconscious patterns (**The Subconscious Oracle - Addendum II**).
- **Application:** Engage in practices like journaling, meditation, and self-reflection to deepen your **Gnosis (Chapter II)** of your own sexuality. This empowers your **Architect of Self (Chapter V)**.

3. **Compassionate Communication (The Weave of Repair):**
    - **Principle:** Engage in open, honest, and empathetic communication with partners about sexual desires, needs, and any challenges that arise.
    - **Application:** Use "I" statements, practice active listening, and approach disagreements with a commitment to understanding and resolution, applying principles from **The Weave of Repair (Addendum XIII)**.

4. **Integration of Shadow Aspects (Balance and Harmony):**
    - **Principle:** Acknowledge and integrate any aspects of your sexuality that have been repressed, shamed, or deemed "unacceptable" (**The Shadow Archetype - Chapter XII**).
    - **Application:** Explore your sexual history and conditioning with self-compassion. Seek to understand the origins of shame or fear, and

consciously work towards acceptance and integration, fostering **Balance and Harmony (Chapter III)**.

5. **Pleasure and Joy (The Luminous Spark):**
    - **Principle:** Embrace pleasure as a natural and healthy aspect of human experience. Sexuality, when consensual and respectful, is a profound source of joy, connection, and vitality.
    - **Application:** Explore what brings you genuine pleasure and connection, both alone and with partners. Celebrate the sensual wisdom of **The Living Vessel (Addendum XII)** and cultivate **The Luminous Spark (Addendum XI)**.

6. **Responsibility and Impact (The Grand Tapestry):**
    - **Principle:** Recognize that sexual choices have ripple effects on individuals, relationships, and the broader community. Practice safe sex and respect the emotional and physical well-being of all involved.
    - **Application:** Take **Responsibility and Agency (Chapter V)** for your sexual health and the impact of your actions. This is a direct application of **Law 4: What You Put Out is What You Get Back (Addendum VII)**.

By embracing **The Sacred Flame of Being** with **Compassion and Reason (Chapter XI)**, practitioners of The Path of Unveiling transform sexuality from a source of potential confusion or shame into a powerful pathway for **Gnosis (Chapter II)**, authentic connection, and profound **Perpetual Becoming (Chapter IV)**, enriching their **Living Vessel (Addendum XII)** and contributing to the vibrant **Grand Tapestry (Chapter I)** of human experience.

Addendum IX: The Great Cycle – Death, Grief, and Mortality on The Path

*Death is the ultimate **Life Transition (Chapter X)**, a universal experience that touches every living being. Yet, in many modern societies, it is often treated with fear, denial, or silence, leading to unresolved grief and a disconnection from life's profound cycles. On **The Path of Unveiling**, we approach death, grief, and mortality not as an end to be feared, but as **The Great Cycle**—an intrinsic, transformative, and sacred part of **The Grand Tapestry (Chapter I)**.*

This addendum explores how to consciously engage with mortality, to honor grief as a natural process, and to find meaning and connection amidst loss. It emphasizes that by embracing death as a part of **The Perpetual Becoming (Chapter IV)**, we can live more fully, cultivate **Compassion and Reason (Chapter XI)**, and deepen our appreciation for the preciousness of existence. It is a profound expression of **The Resonant Echo (Chapter VI)**, connecting us to the universal human experience of loss and renewal.

I. Defining The Great Cycle on The Path
Within The Path of Unveiling, **The Great Cycle** is understood as:

- **The Inherent Cycle of Life and Death:** The natural, continuous process of birth, growth, decay, and transformation that defines all existence, from cosmic phenomena to biological organisms. This aligns with **Law 5: Everything Changes (Except for the First Four Laws)** from **Addendum VII: The Five Laws of Existence**.

- **A Catalyst for Transformation:** Death, while an ending, is also a powerful catalyst for **Transformation and Growth (Chapter IV)**—for the dying, for the bereaved, and for the community. It forces a re-evaluation of values, priorities, and the meaning of life.

- **A Pathway to Deeper Connection:** Consciously engaging with mortality can deepen our appreciation for life, foster more authentic relationships, and strengthen our connection to **The Grand Tapestry (Chapter I)** of all living things.

- **Grief as a Natural Process:** Grief is recognized as a natural, healthy, and necessary response to loss, requiring compassionate acknowledgment and support.

II. The Great Cycle and The Core Tenets of The Path

1. **The Perpetual Becoming:** Death is the ultimate **Transformation and Growth (Chapter IV)**. It is a profound shift in form, allowing for new beginnings and the continuation of energy within **The Grand Tapestry**

(**Chapter I**). It underscores the impermanence of all things, as explored in **The River of Now (Addendum X)**.

2. **The Grand Tapestry:** Death is not separation from, but a return to, **The Interconnectedness of All Being (Chapter I)**. The physical body returns to the Earth, nourishing new life, and the individual's influence and **Resonant Echo (Chapter VI)** remain woven into the collective.

3. **The Ethical Compass:** Approaching death and grief requires profound **Compassion and Reason (Chapter XI)**—both for the dying and for those who mourn. It calls for **Striving for Justice (Chapter XI)** in end-of-life care and for honoring the **Bodily Autonomy (Chapter XI)** of individuals in their final choices.

4. **The Inner Compass:** Facing mortality can be a powerful catalyst for **Gnosis (Chapter II)**, leading to deep insights about the meaning of life, personal values, and the nature of consciousness. It sharpens our focus on what truly matters.

5. **The Architect of Self:** Consciously engaging with one's own mortality empowers **The Architect of Self (Chapter V)** to live a more intentional, purposeful life, making choices that align with deepest values and creating a meaningful **Personal Narrative (Addendum XIX)**.

6. **The Resonant Echo:** The stories, memories, and wisdom of those who have passed continue to resonate through the lives of those they touched, contributing to **The Living Chronicle (Addendum XIX)** and informing future generations.

III. Practices for Embodiment: Navigating The Great Cycle

1. **Mortality Contemplation:**
    - **Practice:** Regularly (e.g., weekly, monthly) dedicate time to quietly contemplate your own mortality. This is not morbid, but a practice of presence. Ask: "If today were my last day, what would I do? What would I say? What would I prioritize?" This aligns with **The River of Now (Addendum X)**.
    - **Purpose:** To cultivate a deeper appreciation for the preciousness of life, to clarify values, and to inspire living with greater intentionality and **Responsibility and Agency (Chapter V)**. This is a powerful form of **Gnosis (Chapter II)**.

2. **Grief Rituals (Secular):**
    - **Practice:** When experiencing loss, create personal or communal rituals to honor grief. This could involve lighting a candle daily, creating a memorial space, writing letters to the deceased, or engaging in a **Life Celebration (Chapter X)**. Allow yourself to feel the emotions of grief without judgment, recognizing it as a natural process. This

is a core aspect of **The Weave of Repair (Addendum XIII)**.
- **Purpose:** To provide a container for processing loss, to acknowledge the pain, and to facilitate the natural movement of grief, fostering **Balance and Harmony (Chapter III)**.

3. **Legacy Reflection and Creation:**
    - **Practice:** Reflect on the legacy you wish to leave—not just material possessions, but the impact of your character, your values, and your contributions to **The Grand Tapestry (Chapter I)**. What kind of **Resonant Echo (Chapter VI)** do you wish to create?
    - **Purpose:** To inspire purposeful living and to consciously shape your **Personal Narrative (Addendum XIX)** as **The Architect of Self (Chapter V)**.

4. **Support for the Bereaved:**
    - **Practice:** Offer compassionate presence and practical support to those experiencing loss within your Hearth or community. Listen without judgment, acknowledge their pain, and offer tangible help.
    - **Purpose:** To embody **Compassion (Chapter XI)** and strengthen the bonds of **The Grand Tapestry (Chapter I)** through mutual support during

challenging times. This is a direct application of **The Weave of Repair (Addendum XIII)**.

5. **Advance Directives and End-of-Life Planning:**
    - **Practice:** Engage in practical planning for your own end of life, including advance directives for medical care, wishes for your body, and instructions for your loved ones. Communicate these clearly.
    - **Purpose:** To exercise **Bodily Autonomy (Chapter XI)** and **Responsibility and Agency (Chapter V)**, easing the burden on loved ones and ensuring your wishes are honored.

By consciously engaging with **The Great Cycle**, practitioners of The Path of Unveiling transform their relationship with death and grief. They cultivate a deeper appreciation for life, live with greater intentionality, and find profound meaning in the continuous **Transformation and Growth (Chapter IV)** that defines all existence within **The Grand Tapestry (Chapter I)**.

Addendum X: The River of Now – The Practice of Time, Presence, and the Flow of Being

*In our fast-paced world, time often feels like a relentless current, dragging us from past regrets to future anxieties. We rush, plan, and worry, frequently missing the richness of the present moment. On **The Path of Unveiling**, we recognize that true power and peace reside not in controlling time, but in consciously engaging with it. This addendum explores **The River of Now**—the profound practice of presence, mindfulness, and aligning with the natural flow of existence.*

*It emphasizes that by anchoring ourselves in the **Eternal Now**, we sharpen **The Inner Compass (Chapter II)**, cultivate **Balance and Harmony (Chapter III)**, and fully embrace our **Responsibility and Agency (Chapter V)** to shape our experience. It is a vital practice for deepening **Gnosis (Chapter II)** and truly living our **Perpetual Becoming (Chapter IV)**.*

I. Defining The River of Now on The Path

Within The Path of Unveiling, **The River of Now** is understood as:

- **The Eternal Present:** The recognition that all existence, all experience, and all potential resides in the present moment. The past is memory, the future is imagination; only the "now" is real. This aligns with **Law 2: Everything is Here and Now** from **Addendum VII: The Five Laws of Existence**.

- **Mindful Presence:** The conscious act of bringing full attention and awareness to whatever is happening in the current moment, without judgment or distraction.

- **Flow of Being:** Aligning with the natural, dynamic, and ever-changing nature of existence, embracing impermanence and the continuous **Transformation and Growth (Chapter IV)**. This connects to **Law 5: Everything Changes (Except for the First Four Laws)** from **Addendum VII**.

II. The River of Now and The Core Tenets of The Path

1. **The Inner Compass:** Presence is the foundation for **Gnosis (Chapter II)**. By being fully present, we can hear the subtle whispers of our intuition and gain direct insight into ourselves and our surroundings. It is how we truly calibrate **The Inner Compass**.

2. **Balance and Harmony:** Anchoring in the present moment helps to balance the mind, reducing anxiety about the future and rumination on the past. It fosters emotional regulation and inner peace, contributing to **The Scales of**

Being (Chapter III) and **The Wellspring Within (Addendum XVIII)**.

3. **The Architect of Self:** Our **Responsibility and Agency (Chapter V)** can only be exercised in the present moment. By being present, we make conscious choices, take intentional actions, and actively shape our reality, rather than being swept away by unconscious patterns. This aligns with **Law 4: What You Put Out is What You Get Back (Addendum VII)**.

4. **The Perpetual Becoming:** Life is a continuous process of **Transformation and Growth (Chapter IV)** that unfolds moment by moment. Embracing **The River of Now** allows us to fully engage with and learn from each stage of our evolution.

5. **The Grand Tapestry:** Presence deepens our connection to **The Interconnectedness of All Being (Chapter I)**. When fully present, we can perceive the intricate details and subtle energies that weave together the fabric of existence, fostering **The Cosmic Reverence (Addendum XIV)**.

6. **The Luminous Spark:** Joy, creativity, and spontaneity often arise from a state of deep presence. Engaging with **The River of Now** allows us to fully experience and cultivate **The Luminous Spark (Addendum XI)** in our lives.

III. Practices for Embodiment: Flowing with The River of Now

1. **Mindful Breathing (Anchor to the Present):**
   - **Practice:** Throughout the day, take short pauses to simply focus on your breath. Notice the sensation of inhale and exhale. When your mind wanders, gently bring it back to the breath. This is a core **Daily Practice (Chapter VII)**.
   - **Purpose:** The breath is always in the present moment, serving as an immediate anchor to **The River of Now**. It's a simple yet powerful way to cultivate **Gnosis (Chapter II)** and calm the nervous system, contributing to **The Wellspring Within (Addendum XVIII)**.

2. **Sensory Immersion:**
   - **Practice:** Choose an ordinary activity (e.g., washing dishes, drinking tea, walking). Engage all your senses fully. Notice the temperature of the water, the scent of the tea, the feeling of your feet on the ground.
   - **Purpose:** To bring full awareness to the present moment, transforming mundane tasks into opportunities for **Gnosis (Chapter II)** and appreciation for **The Living Vessel (Addendum XII)**. This cultivates **The Cosmic Reverence (Addendum XIV)** in everyday life.

3. **"Pause Between" Moments:**
   - **Practice:** Consciously create small pauses throughout your day—before answering the phone, before opening an email, before reacting to a comment. In that brief space, take a breath and choose your response rather than reacting impulsively.
   - **Purpose:** To reclaim **Responsibility and Agency (Chapter V)**, allowing for more intentional and compassionate responses, aligning with **The Ethical Compass (Chapter XI) and Reasoned Error Correction (Chapter XI)**.

4. **Non-Judgmental Observation:**
   - **Practice:** When thoughts or emotions arise, simply observe them without judgment. Acknowledge their presence, but don't get swept away by them. See them as clouds passing in the sky of your mind.
   - **Purpose:** To cultivate **Balance and Harmony (Chapter III)** and emotional regulation, fostering a detached yet aware perspective. This is a key aspect of **The Wisdom of Humility (Addendum XV)**.

5. **Embracing Impermanence:**
   - **Practice:** Reflect on the transient nature of all things—emotions, situations, physical forms. Understand that everything is in a state of

Perpetual Becoming (Chapter IV). This practice is also central to **The Great Cycle (Addendum IX)**.
- **Purpose:** To reduce attachment and suffering, fostering acceptance and resilience. This deepens our understanding of **Law 5: Everything Changes (Except for the First Four Laws)** from **Addendum VII**.

6. **"Future Self" in the Now:**
    - **Practice:** If you have a vision for your "future self" (**The Architect of Self - Chapter V**), ask yourself: "What action can my future self take *right now*?" Bring the desired qualities of your future self into your present actions.
    - **Purpose:** To bridge the gap between aspiration and reality, empowering conscious creation in **The River of Now**.

By consciously flowing with **The River of Now**, practitioners of The Path of Unveiling unlock profound peace, clarity, and vitality. They transform every moment into an opportunity for **Gnosis (Chapter II)**, deepening their **Perpetual Becoming (Chapter IV)**, and living with authentic **Responsibility and Agency (Chapter V)** within **The Grand Tapestry (Chapter I)** of existence.

Addendum XI: The Luminous Spark – The Role of Play, Humor, and Joy on The Path

*In a world often burdened by seriousness, struggle, and the weight of responsibility, the profound importance of **Play, Humor, and Joy** can be easily overlooked. Yet, these are not mere distractions; they are essential wellsprings of vitality, creativity, and resilience. On **The Path of Unveiling**, we recognize these qualities as **The Luminous Spark**—an intrinsic, vital energy that illuminates our **Inner Compass (Chapter II)**, strengthens our **Wellspring Within (Addendum XVIII)**, and deepens our connection to **The Grand Tapestry (Chapter I)**.*

*This addendum explores how to consciously cultivate **The Luminous Spark**, emphasizing its role in fostering **Balance and Harmony (Chapter III)**, fueling **Perpetual Becoming (Chapter IV)**, and enriching every aspect of our human experience. It is a vital practice for living a full, authentic, and truly unveiled life.*

I. Defining The Luminous Spark on The Path
Within The Path of Unveiling, **The Luminous Spark** is understood as:

- **Inherent Vitality:** The innate capacity for joy, curiosity, and spontaneous engagement that resides within every individual.

- **A Catalyst for Growth:** Play and humor are powerful tools for learning, problem-solving, and adapting to change, accelerating **The Perpetual Becoming (Chapter IV)**.

- **An Expression of Balance:** Cultivating joy and lightness balances the necessary seriousness of life, contributing to **The Scales of Being (Chapter III)** and preventing burnout, as discussed in **The Wellspring Within (Addendum XVIII)**.

- **A Pathway to Connection:** Shared laughter and joyful experiences forge deep bonds, strengthening **The Grand Tapestry (Chapter I)** of human relationships.

II. The Luminous Spark and The Core Tenets of The Path

1. **Balance and Harmony: The Luminous Spark** is crucial for maintaining **The Scales of Being (Chapter III)**. It balances introspection with outward expression, effort with ease, and seriousness with levity. Without it, the Path can become overly rigid or draining.

2. **The Perpetual Becoming:** Play encourages experimentation, creativity, and a willingness to embrace the unknown, all vital for **Transformation and Growth**

(**Chapter IV**). Humor helps us navigate challenges with resilience and perspective, transforming obstacles into opportunities for learning (**Reasoned Error Correction - Chapter XI**).

3. **The Inner Compass:** Joy and play can open pathways to **Gnosis (Chapter II)**, fostering intuitive insights and a deeper connection to our authentic selves. When we are joyful, our **Inner Compass** often feels clearer and more aligned.

4. **The Architect of Self:** Consciously choosing to cultivate joy and incorporate play is an act of **Responsibility and Agency (Chapter V)**. It empowers us to intentionally shape our emotional landscape and create a life rich in positive experience.

5. **The Resonant Echo:** Shared stories of joy, humor, and resilience become part of **The Living Chronicle (Addendum XIX)**, creating a **Resonant Echo (Chapter VI)** that inspires and uplifts others. The Trickster archetype (**Chapter XII. Mythological Archetypes**) embodies the disruptive, yet often illuminating, power of humor.

6. **The Wellspring Within:** Play, humor, and joy are essential for replenishing our energetic resources, preventing depletion, and nurturing **The Wellspring Within (Addendum XVIII)**. They are forms of active self-care.

III. Practices for Embodiment: Igniting The Luminous Spark

1. **Conscious Play:**
   - **Practice:** Schedule dedicated time for activities that bring you pure, unadulterated joy and playfulness, without a specific goal. This could be dancing, drawing, playing games, engaging in imaginative activities, or simply being silly.
   - **Purpose:** To reconnect with your innate creativity and spontaneity, releasing stress and fostering **The Luminous Spark**. This is a direct expression of **The Living Vessel (Addendum XII)**.

2. **Cultivating Humor:**
   - **Practice:** Actively seek out sources of humor—comedians, funny stories, lighthearted interactions. Learn to laugh at yourself and life's absurdities. When faced with a challenge, try to find a humorous perspective (without minimizing the difficulty).
   - **Purpose:** Humor provides perspective, reduces tension, and fosters resilience, aiding in **Reasoned Error Correction (Chapter XI)** and navigating **The Weave of Repair (Addendum XIII)**.

3. **Gratitude for Joy:**
   - **Practice:** As part of your **Evening Reflection (Chapter VII. Daily Practices)**, specifically identify moments of joy, laughter, or lightheartedness

from your day. Savor these moments and express gratitude for them.
- **Purpose:** To train your mind to notice and appreciate positive experiences, strengthening **The Wellspring Within (Addendum XVIII)** and cultivating a positive feedback loop.

4. **Embodied Laughter:**
    - **Practice:** Engage in practices that induce laughter, even if initially forced (e.g., laughter yoga, watching funny videos). Notice how laughter physically shifts your state.
    - **Purpose:** Laughter is a powerful physiological release that reduces stress, boosts mood, and connects us to our **Living Vessel (Addendum XII)**.

5. **Spontaneity and Openness:**
    - **Practice:** Allow for moments of unplanned joy or spontaneous action in your day. Be open to unexpected delights and deviations from your routine. This aligns with flowing with **The River of Now (Addendum X)**.
    - **Purpose:** To cultivate adaptability and a playful approach to life, fostering **Perpetual Becoming (Chapter IV)**.

6. **Sharing the Spark:**
    - **Practice:** Share moments of joy and humor with your Hearth or loved ones. Engage in playful

interactions. Your laughter can be contagious, igniting **The Luminous Spark** in others and strengthening **The Grand Tapestry (Chapter I)** of your community.
- **Purpose:** To foster connection, build resilience, and collectively uplift the energy of the community.

By consciously cultivating **The Luminous Spark**, practitioners of The Path of Unveiling ensure their journey is vibrant, joyful, and sustainable. They transform challenges into opportunities for growth, deepen their connections, and illuminate their **Perpetual Becoming (Chapter IV)** with the radiant energy of play, humor, and joy, enriching their own **Wellspring Within (Addendum XVIII)** and contributing to the collective **Grand Tapestry (Chapter I)**.

Addendum XII: The Living Vessel – The Wisdom of the Body and the Senses on The Path

In a world that often prioritizes both the intellect and the abstract, we can easily become disconnected from our most immediate and profound source of wisdom: our own bodies. Our physical form is not merely a container for the mind or spirit; it is a complex, intelligent, and deeply interconnected system, constantly communicating with us through sensations, emotions, and subtle cues. On **The Path of Unveiling***, we recognize the body as* **The Living Vessel**—*a sacred instrument of* **Gnosis (Chapter II)***, a direct connection to* **The Grand Tapestry (Chapter I)***, and a vital partner in our* **Perpetual Becoming (Chapter IV)***.*

This addendum explores how to cultivate a deeper relationship with **The Living Vessel** *and its senses, emphasizing mindful embodiment, intuitive listening, and respectful care. It highlights that by honoring the wisdom of the body, we sharpen* **The Inner Compass (Chapter II)***, foster* **Balance and Harmony (Chapter III)***, and empower our* **Responsibility and Agency (Chapter V)** *in shaping a life of vitality, presence, and authentic* **unveiling***.*

I. Defining The Living Vessel on The Path

Within The Path of Unveiling, **The Living Vessel** is understood as:

- **An Intelligent System:** The body is not just a collection of parts, but a dynamic, self-regulating system with its own innate intelligence and capacity for healing and adaptation. This aligns with **Scientific Understanding (Chapter XI)**, particularly biology and neuroscience (**Chapter XIV. Scientific Insights**).

- **A Conduit for Gnosis:** Through sensations, intuition, and emotional responses, the body provides direct, experiential knowledge that bypasses purely intellectual understanding. It is a primary pathway to **Gnosis (Chapter II)**.

- **Interconnected with All Being:** The body is intimately connected to its environment, constantly exchanging energy and information with **The Grand Tapestry (Chapter I)** of nature and the cosmos.

- **The Seat of Experience:** All our experiences—joy, sorrow, pleasure, pain—are ultimately felt and processed through the body, making it the fundamental ground of our **Perpetual Becoming (Chapter IV)**.

II. The Living Vessel and The Core Tenets of The Path

1. **The Inner Compass:** By cultivating interoceptive awareness (listening to internal bodily cues), we can discern the subtle signals of our **Inner Compass (Chapter II)**, accessing intuitive guidance and a deeper form of **Gnosis**. This is also central to **The Subconscious Oracle (Addendum II)**.

2. **Balance and Harmony:** Honoring **The Living Vessel** involves finding **Balance and Harmony (Chapter III)** between activity and rest, nourishment and detoxification, mental engagement and physical grounding. It also means integrating the physical and non-physical aspects of self.

3. **The Architect of Self:** Conscious care for and listening to **The Living Vessel** is a profound act of **Responsibility and Agency (Chapter V)**. It empowers us to make choices that support our health and well-being, actively shaping our physical reality. This is a core aspect of **The Wellspring Within (Addendum XVIII)**.

4. **The Grand Tapestry:** Our bodies are microcosms of **The Grand Tapestry (Chapter I)**, composed of elements from the Earth and stars, and constantly interacting with the environment. Connecting to the body deepens our sense of belonging to the larger natural world.

5. **The Perpetual Becoming:** The body is in a constant state of **Transformation and Growth (Chapter IV)**, from

cellular renewal to aging. Embracing **The Living Vessel** means accepting and working with these continuous changes.

6. **The Ethical Compass: Bodily Autonomy (Chapter XI)** is a foundational principle for respecting oneself and others. Ethical choices regarding our bodies (e.g., nutrition, movement, sexual expression) also have ripple effects on **The Grand Tapestry (Chapter I)**, connecting to **The Ethical Footprint (Addendum XVI)** and **The Sacred Flame of Being (Addendum VIII)**.

7. **The River of Now:** The body is always in the present moment. Engaging our senses fully is a powerful way to anchor ourselves in **The River of Now (Addendum X)**, cultivating mindfulness and presence.

III. Practices for Embodiment: Listening to the Body's Wisdom

1. **Mindful Movement:**
    - **Practice:** Engage in conscious movement practices such as walking, stretching, yoga, dance, or martial arts. Focus on the sensations in your body, the rhythm of your breath, and the interplay of muscles and joints. This is a core **Daily Practice (Chapter VII)**.
    - **Purpose:** To cultivate body awareness, release tension, and connect to the physical intelligence of **The Living Vessel**. It's a form of active meditation

that grounds you in **The River of Now (Addendum X)**.

2. **Sensory Awakening:**
   - **Practice:** Dedicate time to consciously engage each of your five senses. For example, spend five minutes truly *listening* to the sounds around you, or deeply *smelling* a flower, or mindfully *tasting* a piece of fruit.
   - **Purpose:** To heighten your awareness of the present moment and to receive rich information from **The Grand Tapestry (Chapter I)** through your senses, deepening **Gnosis (Chapter II)**. This also contributes to **The Cosmic Reverence (Addendum XIV)**.

3. **Intuitive Eating and Nourishment:**
   - **Practice:** Listen to your body's hunger and satiety cues. Choose foods that make your **Living Vessel** feel energized and vibrant. Pay attention to how different foods affect your mood and energy levels. This is a key aspect of **Mindful Consumption (Chapter VII)**.
   - **Purpose:** To align your nourishment choices with the wisdom of your body, supporting its optimal functioning and contributing to **The Wellspring Within (Addendum XVIII)**.

4. **Embodied Emotional Awareness:**

- **Practice:** When you experience a strong emotion (e.g., anger, sadness, joy), pause. Instead of immediately reacting or intellectualizing, notice where and how you feel the emotion in your body. Breathe into those sensations.
- **Purpose:** To develop emotional literacy and to understand the body as a messenger of your inner state, fostering **Balance and Harmony (Chapter III)** and aiding in **The Weave of Repair (Addendum XIII)**. This connects to **The Subconscious Oracle (Addendum II)**.

5. **Rest and Rejuvenation:**
   - **Practice:** Prioritize adequate sleep and periods of true rest throughout your day. Listen to your body's signals for fatigue and honor its need for recovery. This is crucial for **The Wellspring Within (Addendum XVIII)**.
   - **Purpose:** To allow **The Living Vessel** to repair, integrate, and replenish its energy, supporting continuous **Perpetual Becoming (Chapter IV)**.

6. **Honoring Bodily Autonomy:**
   - **Practice:** Make conscious choices about your body based on your own **Inner Compass (Chapter II)** and well-being, not external pressures. Respect the bodily autonomy of others in all interactions, particularly in matters of **The Sacred Flame of Being (Addendum VIII)**.

- **Purpose:** To empower your **Responsibility and Agency (Chapter V)** and live in alignment with **The Ethical Compass (Chapter XI)**.

By consciously engaging with **The Living Vessel**, practitioners of The Path of Unveiling unlock a profound source of wisdom and vitality. They deepen their **Gnosis (Chapter II)**, cultivate **Balance and Harmony (Chapter III)**, and navigate their **Perpetual Becoming (Chapter IV)** with greater presence, resilience, and a profound appreciation for the intricate intelligence of their own being within **The Grand Tapestry (Chapter I)**.

Addendum XIII: The Weave of Repair – Navigating Conflict, Forgiveness, and Reconciliation on The Path

Conflict is an inevitable part of the human experience. Whether internal or external, interpersonal or societal, disagreements and harms can fray the delicate threads of **The Grand Tapestry (Chapter I)***. Yet, within every rupture lies an opportunity for deeper understanding, growth, and connection. On* **The Path of Unveiling***, we approach conflict not as something to be avoided at all costs, but as a catalyst for* **The Weave of Repair***—a conscious process of navigating disagreement, practicing forgiveness, and striving for reconciliation.*

This addendum emphasizes that by engaging with conflict through **Compassion and Reason (Chapter XI)***, we strengthen* **The Ethical Compass (Chapter XI)***, foster* **Balance and Harmony (Chapter III)***, and embody our* **Responsibility and Agency (Chapter V)** *in contributing to a more resilient and harmonious* **Grand Tapestry (Chapter I)***. It is a vital aspect of our collective* **Perpetual Becoming (Chapter IV)***.*

I. Defining The Weave of Repair on The Path
Within The Path of Unveiling, **The Weave of Repair** is understood as:

- **A Conscious Process:** It is an intentional, step-by-step approach to addressing disagreements, harms, and misunderstandings, both within oneself and with others.

- **Restorative, Not Punitive:** The focus is on understanding, healing, and restoring relationships, rather than on blame, punishment, or retribution. This aligns with **Reasoned Error Correction (Chapter XI)**.

- **Strengthening Connection:** Paradoxically, when navigated skillfully, conflict can lead to deeper intimacy, trust, and resilience within relationships, reinforcing **The Grand Tapestry (Chapter I)**.

- **Internal and External:** The principles apply to resolving internal conflicts (e.g., self-forgiveness, integrating **The Shadow Archetype - Chapter XII**) as well as external disputes.

II. The Weave of Repair and The Core Tenets of The Path

1. **The Ethical Compass:** This addendum is a direct application of **The Ethical Compass (Chapter XI)**, particularly **Compassion and Reason, Striving for Justice**, and **Reasoned Error Correction**. It provides practical guidance for living these principles in challenging situations.

2. **Balance and Harmony:** Conflict often arises from imbalance. The process of repair seeks to restore **Balance and Harmony (Chapter III)** within individuals and relationships, integrating opposing perspectives and needs. This also relates to integrating **The Shadow Archetype (Chapter XII)**.

3. **Responsibility and Agency:** Engaging in the **Weave of Repair** requires profound **Responsibility and Agency (Chapter V)**. It means owning one's part in the conflict, taking initiative for resolution, and consciously choosing a path of healing. This is an application of **Law 4: What You Put Out is What You Get Back (Addendum VII)**.

4. **The Perpetual Becoming:** Conflict, when navigated constructively, is a powerful catalyst for **Transformation and Growth (Chapter IV)**. It forces individuals and communities to adapt, learn, and evolve, contributing to their continuous **Perpetual Becoming**.

5. **The Grand Tapestry:** The health of **The Grand Tapestry (Chapter I)** relies on the strength of its individual threads. The **Weave of Repair** actively mends frayed connections, strengthening the collective fabric of relationships and community, as seen in **The Unveiling Hearth (Addendum IV)**.

6. **The Inner Compass:** Navigating conflict requires deep introspection and listening to one's **Inner Compass**

(**Chapter II**), discerning truth and identifying underlying needs.

7. **The Living Chronicle:** The process of repair and reconciliation becomes a significant chapter in one's **Personal Narrative (Addendum XIX)** and contributes to the collective **Living Chronicle** of the Hearth.

III. Principles and Practices for The Weave of Repair

1. **Acknowledge and Validate (Compassion and Reason):**
   - **Principle:** Begin by acknowledging that harm or disagreement has occurred and validating the feelings of all parties involved, even if you don't agree with their perspective.
   - **Practice:** Use active listening. Say, "I hear that you are feeling [emotion] because of [situation]." Avoid immediate defensiveness. This is a direct application of **Compassion (Chapter XI)**.

2. **Take Responsibility (Architect of Self):**
   - **Principle:** Identify your own contribution to the conflict, however small. Focus on your actions and intentions, rather than blaming others.
   - **Practice:** Use "I" statements: "I realize my words caused you pain," or "I take responsibility for my part in this misunderstanding." This embodies **Responsibility and Agency (Chapter V)** and **Reasoned Error Correction (Chapter XI)**.

3. **Seek Understanding (Inner Compass & Wisdom of Humility):**
    - **Principle:** Prioritize understanding the other's perspective, needs, and underlying motivations. Assume positive intent where possible.
    - **Practice:** Ask open-ended questions: "Can you help me understand what happened from your point of view?" "What do you need to feel heard/safe/respected?" This requires **The Wisdom of Humility (Addendum XV)** and a willingness to learn.

4. **Communicate with Clarity and Respect (Ethical Compass):**
    - **Principle:** Express your own feelings, needs, and boundaries clearly, calmly, and respectfully, even when emotions are high.
    - **Practice:** Practice non-violent communication techniques. Focus on the behavior, not the person. This applies **Respect for Others' Freedoms (Chapter XI)**.

5. **Forgiveness (Internal and External):**
    - **Principle:** Forgiveness is a process of releasing resentment and anger, primarily for your own well-being. It does not necessarily mean condoning the behavior or forgetting the harm, nor does it require reconciliation. It is a gift you give yourself.

- **Practice:** For internal forgiveness, use journaling or meditation to process emotions and release the need for retribution. For external forgiveness, communicate your willingness to release the burden, if appropriate, without demanding anything in return. This contributes to **The Wellspring Within (Addendum XVIII)**.

6. **Reconciliation (If Appropriate):**
    - **Principle:** Reconciliation is a mutual process of restoring trust and relationship after conflict. It requires both parties to engage in the **Weave of Repair**.
    - **Practice:** If both parties are willing, work collaboratively to establish new agreements, boundaries, and ways of interacting that prevent future harm. This is a practical application of **Balance and Harmony (Chapter III)**.

7. **Learn and Integrate (Perpetual Becoming):**
    - **Principle:** View every conflict as an opportunity for profound learning and **Transformation and Growth (Chapter IV)**.
    - **Practice:** After a conflict is resolved (or even if it's not), reflect on what you learned about yourself, the other person, and the dynamics involved. Integrate these lessons into your **Perpetual Becoming**. This enhances your **Gnosis (Chapter II)**.

By consciously engaging in **The Weave of Repair**, practitioners of The Path of Unveiling transform conflict from a destructive force into a powerful catalyst for deeper connection, personal **Transformation and Growth (Chapter IV)**, and the strengthening of **The Grand Tapestry (Chapter I)** of human relationships, fostering a more resilient and compassionate world.

Addendum XIV: The Cosmic Reverence – The Practice of Awe and Wonder on The Path

In a world saturated with information and distraction, it's easy to lose sight of the extraordinary in the ordinary, the miraculous in the mundane. Yet, the universe itself is a boundless source of beauty, complexity, and mystery, constantly inviting us into states of profound **Awe and Wonder.** *On* **The Path of Unveiling**, *we cultivate* **The Cosmic Reverence**—*a secular, experiential practice of opening ourselves to the magnificence of existence, fostering a deep appreciation for* **The Grand Tapestry (Chapter I)** *and our place within it.*

This addendum emphasizes that cultivating awe is not about belief in the supernatural, but about recognizing the inherent majesty and intricate design of the observable universe and the human spirit. It is a vital practice for sharpening **The Inner Compass (Chapter II)**, *igniting* **The Luminous Spark (Addendum XI)**, *and deepening our* **Gnosis (Chapter II)** *of reality.*

I. Defining The Cosmic Reverence on The Path
Within The Path of Unveiling, **The Cosmic Reverence** is understood as:

- **Secular Awe:** An emotional response to vastness, beauty, or complexity that transcends our current understanding. It is a feeling of profound admiration and respect for the universe and life, without requiring religious belief.

- **Experiential Wonder:** A state of open curiosity and fascination with the natural world, scientific discoveries, human creativity, and the mysteries of consciousness.

- **A Pathway to Gnosis:** Experiencing awe can lead to profound shifts in perspective, a sense of interconnectedness, and intuitive insights that deepen our **Gnosis (Chapter II)**.

- **Connection to The Grand Tapestry:** It is a direct emotional and intellectual engagement with **The Interconnectedness of All Being (Chapter I)**, from the microscopic to the cosmic.

II. The Cosmic Reverence and The Core Tenets of The Path

1. **The Grand Tapestry: The Cosmic Reverence** is the emotional heart of understanding **The Interconnectedness of All Being (Chapter I)**. It is the feeling evoked by recognizing our place within the vast, intricate web of life and the cosmos, as explored in **Addendum I: The Cosmic Tapestry** and **Addendum III: The Path of Light**.

2. **The Inner Compass:** Awe experiences can quiet the ego, broaden perspective, and open us to intuitive insights and a deeper sense of purpose, thereby sharpening **The Inner Compass (Chapter II)** and leading to **Gnosis**.

3. **The Luminous Spark:** Cultivating awe is a direct way to ignite **The Luminous Spark (Addendum XI)**—the inherent joy, vitality, and sense of wonder that enriches life. It fuels creativity and inspiration.

4. **The Perpetual Becoming:** Witnessing the continuous **Transformation and Growth (Chapter IV)** of the universe (e.g., stellar evolution, biological adaptation - **Chapter XIV. Scientific Insights**) inspires a sense of awe at the dynamic nature of existence.

5. **The Wisdom of Humility:** Awe experiences remind us of our small yet significant place in the vastness of the cosmos, fostering **The Wisdom of Humility (Addendum XV)** and an openness to the unknown.

6. **The Resonant Echo:** The universal human capacity for awe and wonder is reflected in art, poetry (**Chapter XV. Poetry and Art**), and philosophical inquiry across cultures, forming a powerful **Resonant Echo (Chapter VI)**.

7. **The Ethical Compass:** A deep reverence for life and the planet can inspire greater **Responsibility and Agency (Chapter V)** in environmental stewardship (**The Ethical**

Footprint - Addendum XVI) and the pursuit of **Striving for Justice (Chapter XI)** for all beings.

III. Practices for Embodiment: Cultivating Awe and Wonder

1. **Nature Immersion:**
    - **Practice:** Spend time in nature with an open, curious mind. Observe the intricate details of a leaf, the majesty of a mountain, the power of the ocean, or the vastness of the night sky. Engage all your senses (**The Living Vessel - Addendum XII**).
    - **Purpose:** Nature is a primary source of awe. This practice deepens your connection to **The Grand Tapestry (Chapter I)** and fosters a profound sense of **Cosmic Reverence.**

2. **Scientific Wonder:**
    - **Practice:** Explore scientific discoveries that reveal the complexity and beauty of the universe—from quantum mechanics to neuroscience, from cosmology to evolutionary biology. Watch documentaries, read articles, or visit science museums.
    - **Purpose:** To cultivate intellectual awe and to ground your sense of wonder in verifiable knowledge, reinforcing **Scientific Understanding (Chapter XI)** and expanding your **Gnosis (Chapter II).**

3. **Art and Music Engagement:**
    - **Practice:** Consciously engage with art, music, or literature that evokes a sense of awe, beauty, or transcendence. Allow yourself to be moved emotionally and intellectually.
    - **Purpose:** To access **The Resonant Echo (Chapter VI)** through creative expression and to ignite **The Luminous Spark (Addendum XI)**. This is explored in **Chapter XV. Poetry and Art**.

4. **Micro-Awe Moments:**
    - **Practice:** Look for small moments of wonder in your daily life: the intricate pattern of a spiderweb, the perfect symmetry of a snowflake, the warmth of the sun on your skin, the complexity of a single cell (as explored in **Chapter XIV. Scientific Insights**).
    - **Purpose:** To train your mind to perceive the extraordinary in the ordinary, cultivating a continuous sense of **Cosmic Reverence** and grounding you in **The River of Now (Addendum X)**.

5. **Contemplation of Scale:**
    - **Practice:** Reflect on the vastness of time (billions of years of cosmic evolution) and space (trillions of galaxies). Then, reflect on the miracle of your own existence—the improbable journey that led to you being here, now.

- Purpose: To foster **The Wisdom of Humility (Addendum XV)** while simultaneously recognizing the profound significance of your individual consciousness within **The Grand Tapestry (Chapter I)**. This connects to **Addendum I: The Cosmic Tapestry**.

6. **Sharing Awe:**
    - **Practice:** Share moments of awe and wonder with others in your Hearth or community. Describe what you experienced and how it made you feel.
    - **Purpose:** To amplify the experience of awe, strengthen communal bonds within **The Unveiling Hearth (Addendum IV)**, and contribute to a collective **Resonant Echo (Chapter VI)** of appreciation for existence.

By consciously cultivating **The Cosmic Reverence**, practitioners of The Path of Unveiling open themselves to the profound beauty and mystery of existence. They deepen their **Gnosis (Chapter II)**, ignite **The Luminous Spark (Addendum XI)**, and live with a heightened sense of appreciation and connection to **The Grand Tapestry (Chapter I)**, enriching their **Perpetual Becoming (Chapter IV)** with boundless awe and wonder.

Addendum XV: The Wisdom of Humility – Embracing Doubt, Uncertainty, and The Unknown on The Path

*In a world that often demands certainty and rewards definitive answers, the courage to embrace **Doubt, Uncertainty, and The Unknown** can feel counterintuitive. Yet, rigid certainty can close us off to new truths, stifle growth, and lead to dogmatism. On **The Path of Unveiling**, we recognize the profound value of this posture, cultivating **The Wisdom of Humility**—a conscious openness to not knowing, a reverence for mystery, and a willingness to revise our understanding in light of new experience.*

This addendum emphasizes that true **Gnosis (Chapter II)** is often found at the edges of our knowledge. By embracing humility, we sharpen **The Inner Compass (Chapter II)**, foster **Balance and Harmony (Chapter III)**, accelerate our **Perpetual Becoming (Chapter IV)**, and strengthen our capacity for **Reasoned Error Correction (Chapter XI)**. It is a vital practice for living authentically and intelligently within **The Grand Tapestry (Chapter I)**.

I. Defining The Wisdom of Humility on The Path

Within The Path of Unveiling, **The Wisdom of Humility** is understood as:

- **Openness to Not Knowing:** A conscious acknowledgment of the limits of our current knowledge and perception, fostering intellectual curiosity rather than dogmatic adherence.

- **Embracing Uncertainty:** The capacity to navigate ambiguity and paradox with equanimity, recognizing that life's deepest truths often defy simple answers. This aligns with **Balance and Harmony (Chapter III)**.

- **Reverence for Mystery:** A profound respect for the aspects of existence that remain beyond our current comprehension, cultivating **The Cosmic Reverence (Addendum XIV)** rather than demanding immediate answers.

- **Intellectual Flexibility:** A willingness to revise beliefs, challenge assumptions, and adapt one's worldview in light of new evidence or experience. This is central to **Reasoned Error Correction (Chapter XI)**.

II. The Wisdom of Humility and The Core Tenets of The Path

1. **The Inner Compass:** Humility is essential for cultivating **Gnosis (Chapter II)**. It allows us to listen more deeply to our intuition, to question our biases, and to remain open

to insights that may challenge our preconceived notions. It ensures our **Inner Compass** is always calibrating.

2. **The Perpetual Becoming:** Embracing doubt and uncertainty is a powerful catalyst for **Transformation and Growth (Chapter IV)**. It forces us to move beyond stagnation, to learn from mistakes (**Reasoned Error Correction - Chapter XI**), and to continuously evolve our understanding. This is vital for **The Living Path (Addendum V)**.

3. **The Ethical Compass:** Humility fosters **Compassion and Reason (Chapter XI)** by encouraging empathy for differing perspectives and a willingness to admit when one is wrong. It is foundational for **Respect for Others' Freedoms (Chapter XI)** and for engaging in **The Weave of Repair (Addendum XIII)**.

4. **The Architect of Self:** A humble **Architect of Self (Chapter V)** recognizes their own fallibility and the limits of their control, leading to more realistic expectations, greater resilience, and a deeper appreciation for the collaborative nature of creation within **The Grand Tapestry (Chapter I)**.

5. **The Grand Tapestry:** Humility connects us more deeply to **The Interconnectedness of All Being (Chapter I)** by dissolving the illusion of individual omniscience and

fostering a sense of shared inquiry within the vastness of existence.

6. **Scientific Understanding (Chapter XI):** The scientific method itself is built on humility—the willingness to test hypotheses, admit when one is wrong, and constantly refine knowledge based on evidence. This is a core part of **The Ethical Compass.**

7. **The Resonant Echo (Chapter VI):** Many **Mythological Archetypes (Chapter XII)** and **Philosophical Excerpts (Chapter XIII)** speak to the wisdom found in embracing the unknown or the limitations of human understanding.

III. Practices for Embodiment: Cultivating Humility

1. **"I Don't Know" Practice:**
    - **Practice:** When faced with a question or a situation where you feel compelled to have an answer, consciously say (to yourself or aloud), "I don't know." Sit with the discomfort of uncertainty.
    - **Purpose:** To build tolerance for ambiguity and to create space for new insights to emerge, rather than prematurely grasping for answers. This sharpens **The Inner Compass (Chapter II).**

2. **The Beginner's Mind:**
    - **Practice:** Approach a familiar task or topic as if you are encountering it for the very first time. Suspend

your assumptions and observe with fresh eyes and open curiosity.
- **Purpose:** To cultivate a receptive state of mind, fostering **Gnosis (Chapter II)** and a willingness to learn from all experiences, accelerating **The Perpetual Becoming (Chapter IV)**.

3. **Seeking Diverse Perspectives:**
   - **Practice:** Actively seek out and listen to viewpoints that differ from your own. Engage in respectful dialogue with people from different backgrounds, cultures, or belief systems.
   - **Purpose:** To challenge your own biases, broaden your understanding of **The Grand Tapestry (Chapter I)**, and practice **Respect for Others' Freedoms (Chapter XI)**. This is crucial for **The Weave of Repair (Addendum XIII)**.

4. **Learning from Mistakes (Reasoned Error Correction):**
   - **Practice:** When you make a mistake, instead of self-judgment or blame, engage in **Reasoned Error Correction (Chapter XI)**. Humbly acknowledge the error, analyze what went wrong, and identify how you can learn and grow from it.
   - **Purpose:** To transform failures into opportunities for **Transformation and Growth (Chapter IV)**, embodying **The Architect of Self (Chapter V)**.

5. **Contemplation of Vastness:**

- **Practice:** Engage in practices that remind you of the immense scale of the universe and the complexity of life (e.g., stargazing, learning about cosmic distances, studying microbiology).
- **Purpose:** To foster **The Cosmic Reverence (Addendum XIV)** and a sense of humility regarding our place within **The Grand Tapestry (Chapter I)**, dissolving the illusion of individual significance.

6. **"Not-Knowing" as a Guiding Principle:**
    - **Practice:** In situations where you feel overwhelmed or unsure, consciously adopt the stance of "not-knowing." Instead of trying to force a solution, allow for intuitive guidance to emerge, trusting your **Inner Compass (Chapter II)**.
    - **Purpose:** To reduce anxiety, foster adaptability, and open yourself to insights from **The Subconscious Oracle (Addendum II)**.

By consciously cultivating **The Wisdom of Humility**, practitioners of The Path of Unveiling navigate life's complexities with greater grace, adaptability, and intellectual honesty. They deepen their **Gnosis (Chapter II)**, accelerate their **Perpetual Becoming (Chapter IV)**, and contribute to a more open, compassionate, and wise **Grand Tapestry (Chapter I)** for all.

Addendum XVI: The Ethical Footprint – Conscious Consumption and Stewardship on The Path

Every choice we make, from the food we eat to the energy we consume, leaves an imprint on the world. In an era of unprecedented global interconnectedness and environmental challenge, understanding this impact is no longer optional; it is an ethical imperative. On **The Path of Unveiling***, we recognize our collective and individual responsibility to cultivate* **The Ethical Footprint***—a conscious approach to consumption and a commitment to stewardship of* **The Grand Tapestry (Chapter I)***.*

This addendum emphasizes that by aligning our actions with **Compassion and Reason (Chapter XI)***, we embody our* **Responsibility and Agency (Chapter V)** *in contributing to a flourishing planet and a just society. It is a vital practice for living our* **Ethical Compass (Chapter XI)** *and accelerating our collective* **Perpetual Becoming (Chapter IV)***.*

I. Defining The Ethical Footprint on The Path
Within The Path of Unveiling, **The Ethical Footprint** is understood as:

- **Conscious Consumption:** Making intentional choices about what we buy, use, and dispose of, considering the environmental, social, and ethical impacts of those choices.

- **Stewardship:** Taking active **Responsibility and Agency (Chapter V)** for the care and preservation of the natural world and its resources, recognizing our role as temporary custodians.

- **Interconnected Impact:** Acknowledging that our individual actions have ripple effects throughout **The Grand Tapestry (Chapter I)**, affecting ecosystems, communities, and future generations. This aligns with **Law 4: What You Put Out is What You Get Back (Addendum VII)**.

- **A Living Expression of Ethics:** It is a practical, daily manifestation of **The Ethical Compass (Chapter XI)**, particularly **Striving for Justice** and **Respect for Others' Freedoms**.

II. The Ethical Footprint and The Core Tenets of The Path

1. **The Grand Tapestry:** This addendum is a direct application of **The Interconnectedness of All Being (Chapter I)**. It highlights how our consumption patterns directly impact the health and balance of ecosystems and human communities globally. It fosters **The Cosmic Reverence (Addendum XIV)** for the Earth.

2. **The Ethical Compass:** The **Ethical Footprint** is a core expression of **The Ethical Compass (Chapter XI)**. It embodies **Compassion and Reason** by seeking to minimize harm, **Striving for Justice** by considering equitable resource distribution, and **Scientific Understanding (Chapter XI)** by relying on evidence-based environmental science (**Chapter XIV. Scientific Insights**).

3. **Responsibility and Agency:** It empowers **The Architect of Self (Chapter V)** to take concrete **Responsibility and Agency (Chapter V)** for their impact on the world, moving beyond passive observation to active contribution.

4. **Balance and Harmony:** Sustainable living is about finding **Balance and Harmony (Chapter III)** between human needs and planetary limits, ensuring resources are used equitably and regeneratively.

5. **The Perpetual Becoming:** Addressing environmental challenges requires continuous **Transformation and Growth (Chapter IV)**, both individually and collectively, in our habits, technologies, and societal structures. It is a long-term commitment to evolving towards a more sustainable future.

6. **The Inner Compass:** Cultivating **The Ethical Footprint** requires listening to our **Inner Compass (Chapter II)**, discerning what truly aligns with our values and what is

truly necessary for flourishing, rather than being driven by external pressures.

7. **The Weave of Repair (Addendum XIII):** Environmental degradation often represents a rupture in **The Grand Tapestry**. Practices of stewardship are acts of **The Weave of Repair**, actively mending and restoring ecological balance.

III. Principles and Practices for The Ethical Footprint

1. **Mindful Consumption (Daily Practice):**
   - **Principle:** Before acquiring anything, pause and ask: "Do I truly need this? What is its origin? What is its impact?" Prioritize needs over wants.
   - **Practice:** Engage in **Mindful Consumption (Chapter VII. Daily Practices)**. Choose products that are ethically sourced, environmentally friendly, and durable. Reduce, reuse, recycle, and repair whenever possible. Support local and sustainable businesses.
   - **Purpose:** To reduce your personal impact and align your daily actions with your values, embodying **The Architect of Self (Chapter V)**.

2. **Resource Conservation:**
   - **Principle:** Conserve natural resources—water, energy, and raw materials—recognizing their

finite nature and their vital role in **The Grand Tapestry (Chapter I)**.
- **Practice:** Reduce energy consumption at home and work. Be mindful of water usage. Support renewable energy initiatives.
- **Purpose:** To contribute to the **Balance and Harmony (Chapter III)** of planetary systems and ensure resources for future generations.

3. **Support for Ethical Systems:**
    - **Principle:** Advocate for and support policies and systems that promote environmental protection, social justice, and sustainable practices on a larger scale.
    - **Practice:** Vote with your values. Support organizations working for environmental and social justice. Engage in peaceful advocacy. This is a direct application of **Striving for Justice (Chapter XI)**.
    - **Purpose:** To extend your **Responsibility and Agency (Chapter V)** beyond personal choices to collective impact, contributing to **The Perpetual Becoming (Chapter IV)** of society.

4. **Connection to Nature (Cosmic Reverence):**
    - **Principle:** Cultivate a deep, experiential connection to the natural world, fostering a sense of reverence and responsibility for its well-being.

~ 253 ~

- **Practice:** Spend regular time outdoors. Learn about local ecosystems. Engage in activities like gardening, hiking, or simply observing nature. This deepens **The Cosmic Reverence (Addendum XIV)**.
- **Purpose:** To inspire a heartfelt commitment to stewardship through direct experience of **The Grand Tapestry (Chapter I)**.

5. **Waste Reduction and Circularity:**
   - **Principle:** Minimize waste production and promote a "circular economy" where resources are continually reused and recycled, rather than discarded.
   - **Practice:** Compost organic waste. Choose products with minimal packaging. Support businesses that have take-back programs or use recycled materials.
   - **Purpose:** To reduce environmental burden and contribute to the regenerative flow of **The Grand Tapestry (Chapter I)**.

6. **Ethical Investment and Divestment:**
   - **Principle:** Align your financial choices with your ethical values, supporting companies and initiatives that demonstrate strong environmental and social responsibility.
   - **Practice:** Research companies' ethical practices. Consider ethical investment funds. Divest from industries that cause significant harm.

- **Purpose:** To extend your **Responsibility and Agency (Chapter V)** into the economic sphere, influencing the broader **Grand Tapestry (Chapter I)**.

By consciously cultivating **The Ethical Footprint**, practitioners of The Path of Unveiling become active stewards of **The Grand Tapestry (Chapter I)**. They embody their **Responsibility and Agency (Chapter V)**, live their **Ethical Compass (Chapter XI)**, and contribute to a more sustainable, just, and flourishing world for all beings, accelerating our collective **Perpetual Becoming (Chapter IV)**.

Addendum XVII: The Guiding Hand – The Transmission of Wisdom, Mentorship, and Learning on The Path

*The journey on **The Path of Unveiling** is deeply personal, yet it is rarely walked alone. Throughout history, wisdom has been transmitted not just through texts, but through the direct exchange between those who have walked a path and those who are just beginning. This addendum explores **The Guiding Hand**—the vital process of **Transmission of Wisdom, Mentorship, and Lifelong Learning** that ensures The Path remains vibrant, accessible, and continuously enriched by collective experience.*

*It emphasizes that sharing and receiving wisdom are acts of **Compassion and Reason (Chapter XI)**, strengthening **The Grand Tapestry (Chapter I)**, and accelerating both individual and collective **Perpetual Becoming (Chapter IV)**. It is a fundamental expression of **The Living Path (Addendum V)**, ensuring its continued evolution and reach.*

I. Defining The Guiding Hand on The Path

Within The Path of Unveiling, **The Guiding Hand** is understood as:

- **Transmission of Wisdom:** The active process of sharing insights, practices, and understanding of The Path from those with more experience to those with less.

- **Mentorship:** A relationship where an experienced practitioner (**Unveiler** or **Keeper**) provides support, guidance, and encouragement to a less experienced individual (**Walker** or **Wanderer**).

- **Lifelong Learning:** A commitment to continuous personal growth, intellectual curiosity, and the integration of new knowledge from all sources, aligning with **Scientific Understanding (Chapter XI)** and **The Wisdom of Humility (Addendum XV)**.

- **A Collective Endeavor:** The responsibility for transmitting wisdom rests not just with designated mentors, but with the entire community of **The Unveiling Hearth (Addendum IV)**.

II. The Guiding Hand and The Core Tenets of The Path

1. **The Perpetual Becoming:** The **Transmission of Wisdom** is essential for continuous **Transformation and Growth (Chapter IV)**, both for the individual receiving guidance and for the evolution of The Path itself (**The Living Path - Addendum V**).

2. **The Grand Tapestry:** Mentorship and shared learning strengthen the bonds within **The Grand Tapestry (Chapter I)**, weaving individuals into a cohesive and supportive community. It ensures the collective wisdom is preserved and expanded.

3. **The Ethical Compass:** Providing guidance is an act of **Compassion (Chapter XI)**. Mentors operate within **The Ethical Compass (Chapter XI)**, upholding **Respect for Others' Freedoms** and empowering the mentee's **Bodily Autonomy (Chapter XI)** and **Responsibility and Agency (Chapter V)**.

4. **The Inner Compass:** Mentors help individuals to sharpen their own **Inner Compass (Chapter II)**, encouraging **Gnosis (Chapter II)** through personal exploration rather than simply providing answers.

5. **The Architect of Self:** Mentorship empowers the mentee to be a more effective **Architect of Self (Chapter V)**, providing tools and perspectives to consciously shape their own path and take **Responsibility and Agency (Chapter V)** for their growth.

6. **The Resonant Echo:** The stories and insights shared through mentorship become part of **The Living Chronicle (Addendum XIX)**, creating a **Resonant Echo (Chapter VI)** that inspires and informs future generations.

7. **The Wisdom of Humility:** Both mentor and mentee embody **The Wisdom of Humility (Addendum XV)**—the mentor by recognizing they don't have all the answers, and the mentee by being open to new perspectives.

III. Roles in The Transmission of Wisdom

1. **The Walker (The Seeker):**
    - **Role:** An individual actively engaged in their personal journey on The Path, seeking to deepen their understanding and practice. They are open to learning and guidance.
    - **Responsibility:** To cultivate their **Inner Compass (Chapter II)**, engage in **Daily Practices (Chapter VII)**, and actively seek knowledge and support. They embody **The Architect of Self (Chapter V)** by taking initiative in their learning.

2. **The Wanderer (The Explorer):**
    - **Role:** An individual who has explored various paths and may be new to The Path of Unveiling, or is in a phase of broad exploration. They bring diverse perspectives.
    - **Responsibility:** To approach The Path with an open mind, to share their unique insights, and to engage in respectful dialogue, contributing to **The Grand Tapestry (Chapter I)**. They embody **The Wisdom of Humility (Addendum XV)**.

3. **The Keeper (The Nurturer of Hearth):**
    - **Role:** An experienced practitioner who takes **Responsibility and Agency (Chapter V)** for nurturing and facilitating an **Unveiling Hearth (Addendum IV)**. They provide a safe space for communal practice and learning.
    - **Responsibility:** To organize gatherings, facilitate discussions, ensure adherence to **The Ethical Compass (Chapter XI)**, and provide initial guidance to new members. Their role is further detailed in **Addendum IV: The Unveiling Hearth**.

4. **The Unveiler (The Guide):**
    - **Role:** A highly experienced and deeply integrated practitioner, certified by **The Council of Unveilers (Addendum VI)**, who provides deeper mentorship and guidance to individuals and groups. They embody profound **Gnosis (Chapter II)** and the principles of **The Living Path (Addendum V)**.
    - **Responsibility:** To offer personalized guidance, facilitate advanced practices, provide wisdom on complex ethical dilemmas, and contribute to the evolution of The Path. They exemplify **The Architect of Self (Chapter V)** and **The Perpetual Becoming (Chapter IV)**.

IV. Practices for Conscious Learning and Mentorship

1. **Active Listening (For Both Mentor and Mentee):**

- **Practice:** When engaged in dialogue, truly listen to understand, rather than to respond. Pay attention to both spoken words and unspoken cues.
- **Purpose:** To foster deep connection, empathy, and effective **Transmission of Wisdom**, aligning with **Compassion and Reason (Chapter XI)** and **The Weave of Repair (Addendum XIII)**.

2. **Question-Based Guidance (For Mentors):**
    - **Practice:** Instead of giving direct answers, guide individuals with insightful questions that encourage them to access their own **Inner Compass (Chapter II)** and find their own **Gnosis (Chapter II)**.
    - **Purpose:** To empower the mentee's **Responsibility and Agency (Chapter V)** and prevent dependency, fostering their growth as an **Architect of Self (Chapter V)**.

3. **Reflective Journaling (For All Roles):**
    - **Practice:** Regularly journal about your learning experiences, insights gained, and challenges faced. If mentoring, reflect on your interactions and how you can better serve.
    - **Purpose:** To integrate knowledge, deepen **Gnosis (Chapter II)**, and contribute to your **Personal Narrative (Addendum XIX)** within **The Living Chronicle (Addendum XIX)**.

4. **Reciprocal Learning:**
    - **Practice:** Recognize that wisdom flows in all directions. Even experienced **Unveilers** can learn from the fresh perspectives of **Walkers** and **Wanderers**.
    - **Purpose:** To embody **The Grand Tapestry (Chapter I)** and **The Wisdom of Humility (Addendum XV)**, fostering a dynamic and continuously evolving **Living Path (Addendum V)**.

5. **Ethical Boundaries in Mentorship:**
    - **Practice:** Mentors maintain clear, respectful, and ethical boundaries, prioritizing the well-being and **Bodily Autonomy (Chapter XI)** of the mentee. They avoid creating dependency or exploiting the relationship.
    - **Purpose:** To ensure that **The Guiding Hand** is always an act of service, aligned with **The Ethical Compass (Chapter XI)**.

By embracing **The Guiding Hand**—both as givers and receivers of wisdom—practitioners of The Path of Unveiling ensure its continued flourishing. They deepen their **Gnosis (Chapter II)**, accelerate their **Perpetual Becoming (Chapter IV)**, and strengthen the vibrant **Grand Tapestry (Chapter I)** of human connection, contributing to a truly **Living Path (Addendum V)** for all.

Addendum XVIII: The Wellspring Within – Sustainable Practice and Self-Care on The Path

*The journey on **The Path of Unveiling** is profound and transformative, requiring consistent engagement, introspection, and ethical action. Without mindful attention to our own energy and well-being, however, even the most dedicated practitioner can experience depletion or burnout. This addendum explores **The Wellspring Within**—the vital practice of **Sustainable Practice and Self-Care**, recognizing that nurturing our inner resources is not selfish, but essential for a vibrant and enduring journey.*

*It emphasizes that by honoring our own needs, we cultivate **Balance and Harmony (Chapter III)**, strengthen our **Responsibility and Agency (Chapter V)**, and ensure our capacity to contribute meaningfully to **The Grand Tapestry (Chapter I)**. It is a fundamental aspect of our **Perpetual Becoming (Chapter IV)** and a direct application of **The Ethical Compass (Chapter XI)** to ourselves.*

I. Defining The Wellspring Within on The Path
Within The Path of Unveiling, **The Wellspring Within** is understood as:

- **Inner Resourcefulness:** The reservoir of physical, emotional, mental, and spiritual energy that sustains our well-being and enables our engagement with The Path.

- **Sustainable Practice:** Engaging with the principles and practices of The Path in a way that is regenerative and prevents depletion, ensuring long-term vitality.

- **Conscious Self-Care:** Intentional actions taken to nourish and replenish oneself, recognizing that personal well-being is foundational to effective action in the world.

- **A Pathway to Balance:** It is the active cultivation of equilibrium between effort and rest, giving and receiving, introspection and outward engagement, aligning with **The Scales of Being (Chapter III)**.

II. The Wellspring Within and The Core Tenets of The Path

1. **Balance and Harmony: The Wellspring Within** is the active cultivation of **The Scales of Being (Chapter III)**. It involves finding the optimal balance between all aspects of life—work, rest, relationships, personal growth—to maintain inner equilibrium.

2. **The Architect of Self:** Prioritizing self-care is a profound act of **Responsibility and Agency (Chapter V)**. It empowers us to consciously manage our energy, make choices that support our well-being, and build a

sustainable foundation for our **Perpetual Becoming (Chapter IV)**.

3. **The Living Vessel:** Self-care practices often involve listening to and honoring the wisdom of **The Living Vessel (Addendum XII)**, attending to its physical needs for rest, nourishment, and movement.

4. **The Luminous Spark:** Nurturing **The Wellspring Within** directly fuels **The Luminous Spark (Addendum XI)**—our capacity for joy, creativity, and vitality. When we are replenished, our inner light shines more brightly.

5. **The Ethical Compass:** Self-care is an ethical imperative. By ensuring our own well-being, we enhance our capacity for **Compassion and Reason (Chapter XI)** towards others and our ability to contribute to **Striving for Justice (Chapter XI)** within **The Grand Tapestry (Chapter I)**. It is a form of **Bodily Autonomy (Chapter XI)** applied to self-preservation.

6. **The Grand Tapestry:** A healthy individual contributes more effectively to the collective. By maintaining our **Wellspring Within**, we strengthen our thread in **The Grand Tapestry (Chapter I)** and increase our capacity to engage in **The Weave of Repair (Addendum XIII)** and **The Ethical Footprint (Addendum XVI)**.

7. **The River of Now:** Self-care often involves anchoring in **The River of Now (Addendum X)**, practicing mindfulness and presence to truly assess and meet our current needs.

III. Practices for Nurturing The Wellspring Within

1. **Mindful Rest and Sleep:**
   - **Practice:** Prioritize adequate, restorative sleep. Create a calming bedtime routine. During the day, take short "micro-rests" or conscious pauses, even just a few deep breaths.
   - **Purpose:** To allow **The Living Vessel (Addendum XII)** to repair and rejuvenate, essential for physical and mental **Balance and Harmony (Chapter III)**. This is a core **Daily Practice (Chapter VII)**.

2. **Conscious Nourishment (Beyond Food):**
   - **Practice:** Pay attention to what truly nourishes you—not just food, but relationships, creative outlets, time in nature, silence, or meaningful work. Conversely, identify what depletes you and consciously limit exposure. This connects to **Mindful Consumption (Chapter VII)**.
   - **Purpose:** To ensure a holistic replenishment of your **Wellspring Within**, fostering **The Luminous Spark (Addendum XI)**.

3. **Setting Boundaries (Architect of Self):**

- **Practice:** Clearly define and communicate your boundaries—with your time, energy, and emotional capacity. Learn to say "no" when necessary, without guilt.
- **Purpose:** To protect your inner resources, exercise **Responsibility and Agency (Chapter V)**, and prevent depletion. This is a vital act of **The Architect of Self (Chapter V)**.

4. **Emotional Processing and Release:**
   - **Practice:** Create regular space for processing emotions through journaling, talking with a trusted friend or therapist, or engaging in cathartic activities (e.g., exercise, creative expression). This aligns with **The Weave of Repair (Addendum XIII)** for internal conflicts.
   - **Purpose:** To prevent emotional buildup that can deplete **The Wellspring Within** and to foster **Balance and Harmony (Chapter III)**.

5. **Connecting to Joy and Play:**
   - **Practice:** Actively seek out activities that bring you pure joy, laughter, and a sense of lightness. Prioritize playfulness in your daily life.
   - **Purpose:** To directly fuel **The Luminous Spark (Addendum XI)** and replenish your energetic reserves, making the journey on The Path sustainable.

6. **Reflection and Adjustment (Perpetual Becoming):**
    - **Practice:** Regularly check in with your **Inner Compass (Chapter II)** to assess your energy levels and overall well-being. Are you thriving or just surviving? Make adjustments to your practices as needed, recognizing that self-care is a dynamic process of **Perpetual Becoming (Chapter IV)**.
    - **Purpose:** To ensure your practices are truly sustainable and responsive to your evolving needs, embodying **Reasoned Error Correction (Chapter XI)**.

7. **Community Support (The Grand Tapestry):**
    - **Practice:** Lean on your **Unveiling Hearth (Addendum IV)** and trusted relationships for support. Offer and receive help. Recognize that asking for help is a strength, not a weakness.
    - **Purpose:** To reinforce that self-care is also a communal act, strengthening **The Grand Tapestry (Chapter I)** through mutual support.

By consciously nurturing **The Wellspring Within**, practitioners of The Path of Unveiling ensure their journey is not only profound but also sustainable and joyful. They embody their **Responsibility and Agency (Chapter V)**, live in **Balance and Harmony (Chapter III)**, and contribute their vibrant energy to the **Grand Tapestry (Chapter I)**, enriching their own **Perpetual Becoming (Chapter IV)** and the collective **Living Path (Addendum V)**.

Addendum XIX: The Living Chronicle – Personal Narrative and Collective Storytelling as Practice on The Path

*Humanity is fundamentally a storytelling species. We define ourselves, make sense of our experiences, and connect with others through the narratives we create and share. On **The Path of Unveiling**, we recognize the profound power of **Personal Narrative and Collective Storytelling** as **The Living Chronicle**—a dynamic, evolving record of our individual and shared journeys of **unveiling**.*

*This addendum emphasizes that consciously crafting and sharing our stories is a vital practice for sharpening **The Inner Compass (Chapter II)**, empowering **The Architect of Self (Chapter V)**, and strengthening **The Grand Tapestry (Chapter I)** of human connection. It is the ultimate expression of **The Resonant Echo (Chapter VI)**, ensuring that wisdom, lessons, and inspiration resonate through time and space.*

I. Defining The Living Chronicle on The Path

Within The Path of Unveiling, **The Living Chronicle** is understood as:

- **Personal Narrative:** The ongoing story we tell ourselves and others about who we are, where we've come from, and where we are going. It shapes our identity and perception of reality.

- **Collective Storytelling:** The shared narratives, myths, and histories that bind communities and cultures, transmitting wisdom and values across generations. This connects directly to **The Resonant Echo (Chapter VI)** and **Mythological Archetypes (Chapter XII)**.

- **A Tool for Gnosis:** By reflecting on and articulating our experiences, we gain deeper insights (**Gnosis - Chapter II**) into our motivations, patterns, and **Perpetual Becoming (Chapter IV)**.

- **Dynamic and Evolving:** The Chronicle is not fixed; it is continuously being written and re-written as we grow, learn, and gain new perspectives. This aligns with **Law 5: Everything Changes (Except for the First Four Laws)** from **Addendum VII: The Five Laws of Existence**.

II. The Living Chronicle and The Core Tenets of The Path

1. **The Resonant Echo:** This addendum is the ultimate expression of **The Power of Story and Symbol (Chapter VI)**. It highlights how narratives, both personal and collective, create a powerful **Resonant Echo** that shapes meaning and transmits wisdom.

2. **The Architect of Self:** Consciously crafting one's **Personal Narrative** is a profound act of **Responsibility and Agency (Chapter V)**. It empowers us to re-author limiting beliefs, define our purpose, and intentionally shape our identity as **The Architect of Self (Chapter V)**.

3. **The Inner Compass:** Storytelling, particularly reflective journaling, helps to clarify our thoughts, feelings, and intuitions, sharpening **The Inner Compass (Chapter II)** and leading to deeper **Gnosis**.

4. **The Perpetual Becoming:** Our lives are continuous stories of **Transformation and Growth (Chapter IV)**. By reflecting on our narratives, we can identify patterns of change, learn from our past, and consciously direct our future **Perpetual Becoming**. This connects to **The Great Cycle (Addendum IX)**, as we integrate life's transitions into our story.

5. **The Grand Tapestry:** Shared stories and collective narratives weave individuals into a cohesive **Grand Tapestry (Chapter I)**. They foster empathy, understanding, and a sense of shared human experience, strengthening **The Unveiling Hearth (Addendum IV)**.

6. **The Ethical Compass:** Stories can transmit ethical principles and inspire moral action. By choosing to tell stories that promote **Compassion and Reason (Chapter XI)**, **Striving for Justice (Chapter XI)**, and **The Weave of**

Repair (**Addendum XIII**), we contribute to a more ethical **Grand Tapestry**.

7. **The Wisdom of Humility:** Recognizing that our **Personal Narrative** is just one thread in a much larger **Grand Tapestry (Chapter I)** fosters **The Wisdom of Humility (Addendum XV)** and an openness to diverse perspectives.

III. Practices for Engaging with The Living Chronicle

1. **Reflective Journaling (Personal Narrative):**
   - **Practice:** Regularly dedicate time to writing about your experiences, thoughts, feelings, and insights. Explore significant events, challenges, and moments of **unveiling**. This is a core **Daily Practice (Chapter VII)**.
   - **Purpose:** To clarify your **Personal Narrative**, gain **Gnosis (Chapter II)** into your patterns, process emotions, and track your **Perpetual Becoming (Chapter IV)**.

2. **"Re-Authoring" Limiting Narratives:**
   - **Practice:** Identify a story you tell yourself that limits you (e.g., "I'm not good enough," "I always fail"). Consciously challenge this narrative. Gather evidence that contradicts it. Write a new, empowering story that reflects your true potential as **The Architect of Self (Chapter V)**.

- Purpose: To exercise **Responsibility and Agency (Chapter V)** in shaping your inner world and overcoming self-imposed limitations. This is a form of **Reasoned Error Correction (Chapter XI)**.

3. **Hearth Story Circles (Collective Storytelling):**
    - **Practice:** Within your **Unveiling Hearth (Addendum IV)**, create dedicated times for sharing personal stories related to specific themes or tenets of The Path. Listen actively and non-judgmentally.
    - **Purpose:** To foster empathy, strengthen communal bonds, and create a collective **Living Chronicle** that enriches **The Grand Tapestry (Chapter I)**. This is a direct application of **The Guiding Hand (Addendum XVII)**.

4. **Engaging with Universal Narratives:**
    - **Practice:** Explore **Mythological Archetypes (Chapter XII)**, **Philosophical Excerpts (Chapter XIII)**, and **Symbolic Language (Chapter XVII)** (like Tarot or Astrology) as universal stories that reflect human experience. Reflect on how these resonate with your own life.
    - **Purpose:** To connect your **Personal Narrative** to the broader **Resonant Echo (Chapter VI)** of human wisdom, gaining deeper insights into universal patterns.

5. **"Future Story" Visualization:**

- **Practice:** Close your eyes and visualize the next chapter of your life as if it were a story already unfolding. What kind of **Architect of Self (Chapter V)** are you? What challenges are you overcoming? What positive impact are you making?
- **Purpose:** To powerfully impress your intentions upon your subconscious (**The Subconscious Oracle - Addendum II**) and align your actions in **The River of Now (Addendum X)** with your desired **Perpetual Becoming (Chapter IV)**.

6. Honoring Ancestral Stories (Secular):
   - **Practice:** Research and reflect on the stories of your biological, cultural, and intellectual ancestors. What lessons, strengths, or challenges did they face? How do their stories resonate with your own?
   - **Purpose:** To deepen your connection to **The Grand Tapestry (Chapter I)** and to understand the **Resonant Echo (Chapter VI)** that precedes and informs your own **Living Chronicle**.

By consciously engaging with **The Living Chronicle**, practitioners of The Path of Unveiling become active co-creators of their own reality and the collective human story. They deepen their **Gnosis (Chapter II)**, empower their **Architect of Self (Chapter V)**, and contribute to a vibrant, ever-unfolding **Grand Tapestry (Chapter I)** of wisdom, connection, and **Perpetual Becoming (Chapter IV)**.

Addendum XX: The Unveiling Process - A Deeper Dive into Personal Transformation

The journey through **The Chronicle of The Path of Unveiling** is, at its core, an invitation to engage with **The Unveiling Process** itself. More than a mere intellectual exercise or a linear progression through information, the Unveiling Process is a dynamic, multi-faceted, and deeply personal odyssey of self-discovery, expansion, and profound alignment with the **Nature of Reality (Chapter VI)**. It is the continuous peeling back of layers—of illusion, conditioning, limiting beliefs, and unconscious patterns—to reveal the inherent truth, wisdom, and potential that resides within each individual and within the fabric of all existence.

This process is not about acquiring something new, but rather about remembering and revealing what has always been present. It is a re-awakening of the **Inner Compass (Chapter II)**, a refinement of our capacity for **Gnosis**, and a courageous embrace of our **Responsibility and Agency (Chapter V)** as **Architects of Self**. The Unveiling is characterized by cycles of expansion and contraction, challenge and insight, prompting continuous **Transformation and Growth (The Perpetual Becoming, Chapter IV)**. It demands **Awareness (Chapter VII)**—a mindful presence that allows us to perceive what is truly unfolding, both internally and externally. As we unveil, we become more attuned to the subtle energies of **The Grand Tapestry (Chapter I)**, recognizing the profound **Interconnectedness of All Being**. This deepens our capacity for **Balance and Harmony (Chapter III)**, not as a static state, but as a dynamic equilibrium that adjusts to the ever-present flow of **The River of Now (Addendum X)**.

Crucially, the Unveiling Process is inherently linked to the integration of **The Language of Light and Shadow (Addendum XXV)**, acknowledging and harmonizing all aspects of our being for true wholeness. It is propelled by **The Power of Intent (Chapter VIII)**, where conscious direction guides our evolution, always in alignment with **The Ethical Compass (Chapter XI)** for the highest good. As we navigate this path, we often encounter **Life Transitions (Chapter X)**, which serve as catalysts for deeper understanding and offer opportunities for **Healing and Restoration (Chapter IX)**. The wisdom gleaned from our unfolding experiences contributes to **The Living Chronicle (Addendum XIX)**, the evolving testament of collective human wisdom. Ultimately, the Unveiling Process culminates in the harmonious integration of all aspects of self, forming **The Symphony of Self (Addendum XXVIII)**, and preparing us for conscious participation in **The Global Hearth (Addendum XXIX)**—a unified future born from individual and collective awakening.

The Unveiling Process is therefore the very essence of living an awakened life. It is the active engagement with our inherent potential, a commitment to truth, and an ongoing dance with the mysteries of existence. It is the path of conscious evolution, leading us ever closer to our most authentic self and our rightful place within the grand design.

Addendum XXI: The Hearth – The Practice of Cultivating Authentic Connection

Within the vast tapestry of existence, while the journey of Unveiling is deeply personal, it is rarely a solitary one. Humanity thrives on connection, on the shared warmth and mutual support that binds individuals into a collective. This foundational truth is embodied in **The Hearth** – a symbolic and literal space representing the authentic connections we cultivate with others, whether they be family, friends, or a consciously chosen community of like-minded souls. It is here, within the safety and resonance of The Hearth, that individual Unveiling is amplified, challenges are softened, and the richness of shared experience deepens our collective understanding of **The Grand Tapestry (Chapter I)**.

The Hearth is more than just a gathering place; it is a dynamic ecosystem of **authentic connection**. This authenticity arises from a commitment to vulnerability, empathy, and mutual respect, fostering an environment where individuals feel seen, heard, and valued for their true selves. It is a space where the principles of **Balance and Harmony (Chapter III)** are lived out in interpersonal dynamics, where **The Ethical Compass (Chapter XI)** guides interactions, and where **Healing and Restoration (Chapter IX)** can occur through compassionate presence. Within The Hearth, the unique **Inner Compass (Chapter II)** of each individual is honored, allowing for diverse perspectives to contribute to a richer collective **Gnosis**.

Cultivating The Hearth involves active engagement in practices that nurture these bonds: shared inquiry, compassionate communication, offering and receiving support, celebrating successes, and navigating challenges together. It recognizes that our individual **Transformation and Growth (The Perpetual Becoming, Chapter IV)** is intricately linked to the well-being of our connections. As we grow, our capacity for connection expands, reaching beyond our immediate circle to encompass a broader sense of kinship with all beings, laying the groundwork for the eventual manifestation of **The Global Hearth (Addendum XXIX)**. The strength of these authentic connections provides vital resilience during **Life Transitions (Chapter X)** and serves as a profound source of **The Luminous Spark (Addendum XI)** – the joy and aliveness that comes from true belonging. Ultimately, The Hearth is a living testament to the truth that we are **Interconnected (Chapter I)**, and that our greatest strength lies in our capacity to come together, to share our light, and to collectively unveil the profound beauty of our shared existence.

Addendum XXII: The Role of Ritual and Ceremony - *Crafting Meaning through Intentional Action*

Humanity has, since its earliest stirrings, instinctively engaged with **Ritual and Ceremony**. These are not mere superstitions or archaic practices, but profound, intentional acts designed to mark transitions, imbue meaning, connect with the sacred, and anchor consciousness within the ever-unfolding narrative of existence. In **The Chronicle of The Path of Unveiling**, Ritual and Ceremony serve as powerful catalysts and anchors for the **Unveiling Process (Addendum XX)**, providing structure and profound resonance to individual and collective transformation. They are conscious frameworks that help us navigate the seen and unseen layers of **The Nature of Reality (Chapter VI)**.

Rituals and ceremonies, whether personal and quiet or communal and grand, are expressions of **The Power of Intent (Chapter VIII)** made manifest. They create sacred space, focus **Awareness (Chapter VII)**, and provide a container for deep emotional and spiritual processing. By engaging the body, mind, and spirit, they help to integrate shifts that occur during **Life Transitions (Chapter X)**, transforming moments of change into meaningful **Cycles of Becoming**. These practices can facilitate **Healing and Restoration (Chapter IX)** by providing a structured way to release old patterns, grieve losses, or celebrate new beginnings. They bridge the gap between our inner **Gnosis (Chapter II)** and outer expression, making abstract truths tangible and accessible.

The regular practice of ritual, such as daily meditation (**Chapter VII. Daily Practices** or **Addendum XIV: The Cosmic Reverence – The Practice of Awe and Wonder on The Path**) or mindful breathwork, cultivates consistent **Balance and Harmony (Chapter III)** within the individual. Communal ceremonies, on the other hand, strengthen **The Hearth (Addendum XXI)** by fostering **authentic connection** and a shared sense of purpose. They reinforce **The Interconnectedness of All Being (Chapter I)**, reminding participants of their place within **The Grand Tapestry**. Through their symbolic language and repetitive nature, rituals embed universal truths and **Mythological Archetypes (Chapter XII)** into the collective psyche, shaping **The Living Chronicle (Addendum XIX)**. Ultimately, the conscious application of Ritual and Ceremony empowers us to actively participate in our **Transformation and Growth (The Perpetual Becoming, Chapter IV)**, aligning our personal and collective journey with **Universal Law (Addendum XXX)** and enriching the very fabric of our unfolding reality.

Addendum XXIII: The Ethical Compass - Applying Principles to Artificial Intelligence & Emerging Technologies

As humanity accelerates its **Unveiling Process (Addendum XX)** and its capacity for creation, the emergence of **Artificial Intelligence (AI) and other Emerging Technologies** presents both unprecedented opportunities and profound ethical considerations. This Addendum expands upon the **Principles of The Ethical Compass (Chapter XI)**, applying its timeless wisdom to the rapidly evolving landscape of advanced technology. The challenge is to ensure that these powerful tools are developed and utilized in alignment with the highest good of all beings and **The Grand Tapestry (Chapter I)**, rather than inadvertently creating new forms of imbalance or fragmentation.

The ethical development of AI and emerging technologies demands a deep commitment to principles such as **Responsibility and Agency (Chapter V)**, recognizing that we are the **Architects of Self** and, by extension, the architects of the technological future we are co-creating. This means consciously embedding values like fairness, transparency, and accountability into algorithms and systems from their inception. It requires a profound understanding of **The Interconnectedness of All Being (Chapter I)**, acknowledging that technological advancements impact not only human societies but also the natural world and the delicate **Balance and Harmony (Chapter III)** of ecosystems. **The Practice of Discernment (Addendum XXVII)** becomes paramount, allowing us to critically evaluate potential benefits against risks, and to differentiate between innovation that serves true progress and that which merely amplifies existing societal shadows.

Furthermore, the integration of AI and emerging technologies must be guided by **Gnosis (Chapter II)**, ensuring that technological intelligence complements and enhances human wisdom, rather than supplanting it. We must strive to use these tools to augment our capacity for **Healing and Restoration (Chapter IX)**, to foster **Collective Intelligence and Consciousness (Addendum II: The Subconscious Oracle – Accessing Inner Wisdom and Parallel Realities)** and to accelerate the compassionate transition towards **The Global Hearth (Addendum XXIX)**. This requires ongoing dialogue, a willingness to adapt, and a continuous recalibration of our Ethical Compass as technology evolves. The ultimate aim is to wield these powerful creations with foresight, humility, and a steadfast commitment to **Universal Law (Addendum XXX)**, ensuring they become instruments of our collective **Transformation and Growth (The Perpetual Becoming, Chapter IV)**, serving to uplift and unite all life within **The Living Chronicle (Addendum XIX)**.

Addendum XXIV: The Power of Story and Narrative - *Shaping Reality through Conscious Storytelling*

From the earliest cave paintings to the sprawling digital epics of today, humanity has been defined by **The Power of Story and Narrative**. This Addendum delves into how stories are not merely entertainment but fundamental vehicles for conveying meaning, transmitting wisdom, shaping cultural understanding, and anchoring our individual and collective **Unveiling Process (Addendum XX)**. Stories provide the frameworks through which we interpret **The Nature of Reality (Chapter VI)**, understand ourselves, and envision our future.

Stories act as living bridges, connecting us to **Mythological Archetypes (Chapter XII)** that resonate deeply within the human psyche. They allow us to explore complex truths, grapple with **The Language of Light and Shadow (Addendum XXV)**, and process the profound lessons embedded within **Life Transitions (Chapter X)**. Through narrative, abstract principles like **The Interconnectedness of All Being (Chapter I)** become relatable, and the intricacies of **Universal Law (Addendum XXX)** are revealed through their observable consequences in a character's journey. By engaging with stories, we can cultivate **empathy**, expand our **Awareness (Chapter VII)**, and access a form of indirect **Gnosis (Chapter II)** that bypasses purely intellectual understanding, settling instead into the heart.

Crucially, **The Power of Story and Narrative** empowers us to become conscious contributors to **The Living Chronicle (Addendum XIX)**. Each individual life is a unique narrative, and by consciously shaping our personal stories—revising limiting beliefs, embracing our **Responsibility and Agency (Chapter V)**, and articulating our **Intent (Chapter VIII)**—we actively participate in our own **Transformation and Growth (The Perpetual Becoming, Chapter IV)**. Furthermore, the collective stories we tell and perpetuate influence the trajectory of **The Global Hearth (Addendum XXIX)**, emphasizing the ethical imperative of crafting narratives that promote **Balance and Harmony (Chapter III)**, **Healing and Restoration (Chapter IX)**, and the highest good for all. Recognizing the profound impact of narrative, both personal and societal, grants us a potent tool for conscious evolution, enabling us to weave a future aligned with truth and compassion.

Addendum XXV: The Language of Light and Shadow - *Integrating the Duality of Self and Psyche*

Life, in its profound complexity, often presents itself as a dance of opposites: joy and sorrow, strength and vulnerability, creation and destruction. This Addendum explores **The Language of Light and Shadow**, recognizing that these seemingly opposing forces are not inherently good or bad, but rather integral aspects of existence that comprise the totality of being. Light represents conscious awareness, integrated qualities, and expressed potential, while Shadow encompasses the unconscious, disowned, or unexpressed aspects of self and reality. Mastering this language is crucial for true **Balance and Harmony (Chapter III)** and for accelerating the **Unveiling Process (Addendum XX)**.

The journey into Light and Shadow demands courage and an unwavering commitment to self-discovery, fueled by deep **Gnosis (Chapter II)**. It requires us to bring **Awareness (Chapter VII)** to those parts of ourselves—our fears, insecurities, past traumas, or even unacknowledged strengths—that reside in the metaphorical shadow, often influencing our actions from an unconscious realm. This process of acknowledgment and integration is fundamental to **Healing and Restoration (Chapter IX)**, as it reclaims fragmented aspects of the self, moving us towards wholeness. By understanding the interplay of Light and Shadow, we gain profound insight into **Mythological Archetypes (Chapter XII)** and the universal patterns that manifest in human experience, both individually and collectively.

Embracing **The Language of Light and Shadow** empowers us to wield our **Responsibility and Agency (Chapter V)** more consciously. When we integrate our shadow, we make choices from a place of wholeness rather than unconscious reaction, aligning our **Power of Intent (Chapter VIII)** with our authentic self and **The Ethical Compass (Chapter XI)**. This continuous process of integration is a core aspect of **Transformation and Growth (The Perpetual Becoming, Chapter IV)**, enabling us to transcend duality and embody a more complete expression of ourselves within **The Grand Tapestry (Chapter I)**. It teaches us that true luminosity is not the absence of darkness, but the courageous integration of all that we are, allowing the full spectrum of our being to contribute to **The Living Chronicle (Addendum XIX)** and the unfolding of **Universal Law (Addendum XXX)**.

Addendum XXVI: The Role of Play and Creativity - *Fostering Innovation and Joyful Unveiling*

In a world often characterized by seriousness, productivity, and relentless pursuit, **The Role of Play and Creativity** might seem frivolous. Yet, this Addendum asserts that engaging in conscious play and fostering uninhibited creativity are not mere pastimes, but essential, powerful practices for accelerating the **Unveiling Process (Addendum XX)**. They are vital conduits for accessing profound **Gnosis (Chapter II)**, fostering adaptability, and maintaining the **Balance and Harmony (Chapter III)** necessary for true **Transformation and Growth (The Perpetual Becoming, Chapter IV)**.

Play, in its purest form, is spontaneous, joyful, and often without a predetermined outcome. It allows for experimentation, failure without judgment, and the free exploration of possibilities. This very nature makes it a profound teacher in understanding **The Nature of Reality (Chapter VI)**, particularly its fluid and emergent aspects. Creativity, an extension of play, is the inherent human capacity to bring new ideas, forms, and solutions into existence, whether through traditional arts (**Chapter XV: Poetry and Art**) or innovative problem-solving in daily life. Both ignite the **Luminous Spark**

(**Addendum XI**) within, fostering vitality and a deeper connection to the innate joy of existence.

Consciously embracing **The Role of Play and Creativity** cultivates an expansive sense of **Awareness (Chapter VII)**, allowing us to see beyond rigid structures and perceive novel connections within **The Grand Tapestry (Chapter I)**. It enhances our **Responsibility and Agency (Chapter V)** by empowering us to playfully experiment with different choices and outcomes, refining our **Power of Intent (Chapter VIII)**. Moreover, play can be a powerful tool for **Healing and Restoration (Chapter IX)**, providing a safe space to process emotions, release tension, and reintegrate fragmented aspects of self, including those revealed through **The Language of Light and Shadow (Addendum XXV)**. By integrating play and creativity into our daily lives, we align with the natural, evolving rhythms of **Universal Law (Addendum XXX)**, becoming more resilient, innovative, and joyful contributors to **The Living Chronicle (Addendum XIX)** and the unfolding story of **The Global Hearth (Addendum XXIX)**.

Addendum XXVII: The Practice of Discernment - *Perceiving Truth in a Complex World*

In a world saturated with information, conflicting narratives, and myriad pathways, the ability to perceive truth amidst illusion becomes not just a skill, but a spiritual imperative. **The Practice of Discernment** is the cultivated capacity to perceive with clarity, to distinguish between what genuinely serves one's highest good and the well-being of **The Grand Tapestry (Chapter I)**, and what does not. It is an active engagement of **The Inner Compass (Chapter II)**, refined by **Gnosis**, to navigate the complexities of **The Nature of Reality (Chapter VI)** and make choices that align with **Universal Law (Addendum XXX)**.

Discernment is far more than intellectual analysis; it is an intuitive and holistic process that integrates mind, heart, and spirit. It involves listening to the subtle whispers of intuition, observing patterns, and evaluating information not just for its logical coherence, but for its energetic resonance and its alignment with core principles of **Interconnectedness, Balance and Harmony (Chapter III)**, and **The Ethical Compass (Chapter XI)**. It empowers **Responsibility and Agency (Chapter V)**, allowing individuals to consciously choose their beliefs, actions, and associations, rather than being swayed by external pressures or unconscious biases. The practice helps us to recognize the subtle workings of **The Language of Light and Shadow (Addendum XXV)**, ensuring that we integrate insights rather than being misled by unexamined aspects of self or others.

Cultivating **The Practice of Discernment** requires consistent **Awareness (Chapter VII)** through **Daily Practices**, a willingness to question assumptions, and the courage to shift perspective when new information arises. It is essential for navigating **Life Transitions (Chapter X)**, where clarity is often obscured by uncertainty, and for applying **The Power of Intent (Chapter VIII)** effectively towards beneficial creation. In an age of rapidly emerging technologies, particularly **Artificial Intelligence (Addendum XXIII: The Ethical Compass - Artificial Intelligence & Emerging Technologies)**, discernment becomes crucial for discerning authentic information from engineered illusion. Ultimately, through diligent discernment, we refine our personal **Transformation and Growth (The Perpetual Becoming, Chapter IV)** and contribute to the collective **Unveiling Process (Addendum XX)**, enriching **The Living Chronicle (Addendum XIX)** with wisdom grounded in clarity and truth.

Addendum XXVIII: The Symphony of Self - *The Integration of All Aspects of Being*

The individual journey of **Unveiling (Addendum XX)** culminates not in a singular destination, but in the harmonious integration of all aspects of being, leading to **The Symphony of Self**. This Addendum explores the profound state where the myriad dimensions of an individual—physical, emotional, mental, spiritual, and energetic—resonate together in a dynamic and coherent whole. It is the conscious realization that each person is a unique, living composition within **The Grand Tapestry (Chapter I)**, contributing a distinct and essential note to the cosmic melody.

Achieving **The Symphony of Self** is a direct outcome of diligently engaging with **The Unveiling Process (Addendum XX)**. It stems from cultivating **Balance and Harmony (Chapter III)** across all internal landscapes, allowing the diverse instruments of our being to play in concert rather than discord. This involves deep **Healing and Restoration (Chapter IX)**, integrating the fragmented notes of past wounds and **The Language of Light and Shadow (Addendum XXV)** into a unified composition. It is propelled by **Transformation and Growth (The Perpetual Becoming, Chapter IV)**, where each cycle of expansion and refinement adds richness and complexity to our unique melodic line. The clarity of **The Inner Compass (Gnosis, Chapter II)** acts as the conductor, guiding the individual's expression in alignment with their authentic truth and **Universal Law (Addendum XXX)**.

When an individual embodies **The Symphony of Self**, their **Responsibility and Agency (Chapter V)** become deeply aligned with their intrinsic purpose. Their **Power of Intent (Chapter VIII)** resonates with authenticity, creating ripples of positive influence within **The Hearth (Addendum XXI)** and beyond. Their daily **Awareness (Chapter VII)** becomes a mindful presence, allowing them to perceive the intricate beauty of their own composition and the interconnectedness of all musical movements within existence. This state is marked by an effortless flow, a radiant presence, and a profound sense of inner peace and aliveness—**The Luminous Spark (Addendum XI)**. Ultimately, **The Symphony of Self** is the individual's highest contribution to **The Living Chronicle (Addendum XIX)**, serving as an inspiring resonance that uplifts and informs the ongoing creation of **The Global Hearth (Addendum XXIX)**. It is the conscious embodiment of divine artistry, living proof that each being is a masterpiece in continuous creation.

Addendum XXIX: The Global Hearth - A Vision for a Unified and Conscious Humanity

While the journey of Unveiling begins intimately within the individual, its ultimate trajectory leads to a profound expansion of consciousness and a recognition of shared destiny embodied in **The Global Hearth**. This pivotal Addendum envisions a future state of conscious humanity, characterized by universal **Interconnectedness (Chapter I)**, collective **Balance and Harmony (Chapter III)**, and a shared commitment to the highest good of all life on Earth and beyond. It is the grand culmination of individual **Unveiling Process (Addendum XX)** contributing to a unified collective.

The Global Hearth transcends geographical boundaries, cultural differences, and historical divisions. It is a metaphorical space where the principles of **The Ethical Compass (Chapter XI)** are universally applied, guiding collective **Responsibility and Agency (Chapter V)** towards sustainable living, equitable resource distribution, and peaceful coexistence. It represents a state where humanity's diverse **Symphonies of Self (Addendum XXVIII)** resonate in exquisite harmony, each unique note contributing to a grander cosmic composition. The establishment of The Global Hearth necessitates a profound shift in collective **Awareness (Chapter VII)**, recognizing our shared vulnerability and interdependence within **The Grand Tapestry**.

Achieving **The Global Hearth** requires a conscious application of **The Power of Intent (Chapter VIII)** on a planetary scale, directing our collective will towards solutions that serve the entire ecosystem. It draws upon the wisdom gained through navigating countless **Life Transitions (Chapter X)**, both individual and societal, and integrates the lessons learned from **Healing and Restoration (Chapter IX)** of historical wounds and environmental imbalances. The continuous **Transformation and Growth (The Perpetual Becoming, Chapter IV)** of humanity will be marked by a deepening collective **Gnosis (Chapter II)**, informed by **Scientific Insights (Chapter XIV)** and expressed through **The Power of Story and Narrative (Addendum XXIV)** that promote unity and shared purpose.

The conscious integration of **The Language of Light and Shadow (Addendum XXV)** on a global scale will allow humanity to confront its collective shadow and emerge into a brighter, more integrated future. Ultimately, The Global Hearth is the living testament to **Universal Law (Addendum XXX)** manifesting as conscious co-creation, where humanity, as a unified force, becomes a responsible steward of its planetary home and a conscious participant in the greater cosmic unfolding, continually writing **The Living Chronicle (Addendum XIX)**.

Addendum XXX: Universal Law - Aligning with the Fundamental Principles of Existence

Beyond the myriad expressions of reality, underlying all phenomena, and orchestrating the dance of existence, lie **Universal Laws**. This Addendum posits that these are not human constructs or dogmas, but fundamental, immutable principles that govern the cosmos, from the smallest subatomic particle to the grandest galaxy, and from the unfolding of a single thought to the evolution of civilizations. Understanding and aligning with these laws is paramount to navigating the **Unveiling Process (Addendum XX)**, achieving true **Balance and Harmony (Chapter III)**, and realizing our authentic place within **The Grand Tapestry (Chapter I)**.

Universal Laws operate ceaselessly, whether we are conscious of them or not. They are the unseen architecture upon which **The Nature of Reality (Chapter VI)** is built, and they provide the framework for our **Transformation and Growth (The Perpetual Becoming, Chapter IV)**. Principles such as cause and effect (karma), resonance, attraction, polarity, rhythm, and perpetual transmutation are not merely philosophical concepts but observable forces that shape our experiences. **Scientific Insights (Chapter XIV)**, particularly from fields like quantum physics, cosmology, and systems theory, increasingly reveal the elegant consistency and interconnectedness of these laws as they manifest in the physical world, offering empirical validation for ancient wisdom.

Embracing **Universal Law** demands a profound shift in **Awareness (Chapter VII)** and a deep commitment to **The Practice of Discernment (Addendum XXVII)**. It calls us to refine our **Inner Compass (Gnosis, Chapter II)** to perceive these underlying patterns and to wield our **Responsibility and Agency (Chapter V)** in conscious alignment with them. When our **Power of Intent (Chapter VIII)** is harmonized with Universal Law, our capacity for positive creation and manifestation is amplified. When we act in accordance with these immutable principles, our choices naturally align with **The Ethical Compass (Chapter XI)**, contributing to the highest good for ourselves and for **The Global Hearth (Addendum XXIX)**. By actively studying, observing, and integrating Universal Law into our lives, we transcend the illusion of separation and become conscious participants in the cosmic symphony, truly embodying **The Living Chronicle (Addendum XIX)** as we contribute to the ever-unfolding story of creation.

I. References for "The Chronicle of The Path of Unveiling" (Main Text)

For Interconnectedness (The Grand Tapestry - Chapter I) & Systems Thinking:
- Capra, Fritjof. *The Web of Life: A New Scientific Understanding of Living Systems.* Anchor Books, 1996.
  - **Relevance:** A foundational text on systems theory and ecology, explaining interconnectedness from a scientific perspective. Directly supports "Modern Resonances" in Chapter I and **The Ethical Footprint (Addendum XVI)**.
- Lovelock, James. *Gaia: A New Look at Life on Earth.* Oxford University Press, 1979.
  - **Relevance:** Introduces the Gaia hypothesis, viewing Earth as a self-regulating, interconnected system. Reinforces **The Grand Tapestry** and **The Ethical Footprint**.

For Gnosis/Inner Wisdom (The Inner Compass - Chapter II) & Mindfulness/Psychology:
- Kabat-Zinn, Jon. *Wherever You Go, There You Are: Mindfulness Meditation in Everyday Life.* Hyperion, 1994.

- Relevance: A classic on secular mindfulness, directly supporting practices for cultivating **The Inner Compass** and presence (**The River of Now - Addendum X**).
- Jung, Carl G. *Man and His Symbols*. Dell Publishing, 1964.
  - Relevance: Explores the power of archetypes and the collective unconscious, providing a psychological framework for **The Resonant Echo (Chapter VI)**, **Mythological Archetypes (Chapter XII)**, and **Symbolic Language (Chapter XVII)**.
- Daniel Kahneman. *Thinking, Fast and Slow*. Farrar, Straus and Giroux, 2011.
  - Relevance: Explores cognitive biases and the two systems of thinking (intuitive and rational), which can inform the cultivation of **The Inner Compass** and **Reason (Chapter XI)**.

For Balance and Harmony (The Scales of Being - Chapter III) & Well-being:

- Csikszentmihalyi, Mihaly. *Flow: The Psychology of Optimal Experience*. Harper Perennial, 1990.
  - Relevance: Explores the concept of "flow" states, where individuals experience deep engagement and balance, directly supporting **The Scales of Being** and **The Luminous Spark (Addendum XI)**.
- Neff, Kristin. *Self-Compassion: The Proven Power of Being Kind to Yourself*. William Morrow, 2011.

- **Relevance:** Provides a secular, research-backed approach to self-compassion, crucial for **Balance and Harmony** and **The Wellspring Within** (Addendum XVIII).

For Transformation and Growth (The Perpetual Becoming - Chapter IV) & Resilience:

- Dweck, Carol S. *Mindset: The New Psychology of Success.* Random House, 2006.
  - **Relevance:** Introduces the concept of "growth mindset," aligning with **The Perpetual Becoming** and **Reasoned Error Correction (Chapter XI)**.
- Frankl, Viktor E. *Man's Search for Meaning.* Beacon Press, 1959.
  - **Relevance:** Explores finding meaning amidst suffering and the human capacity for resilience and transformation, highly relevant to **The Perpetual Becoming** and **The Great Cycle** (Addendum IX).

For Responsibility and Agency (The Architect of Self - Chapter V) & Ethics:

- Pigliucci, Massimo. *How to Be a Stoic: Ancient Wisdom for Modern Living.* Basic Books, 2017.
  - **Relevance:** A contemporary interpretation of Stoicism, directly supporting **The Architect of Self** and **The Ethical Compass (Chapter XI)**.
- Harris, Sam. *Moral Landscape: How Science Can Determine Human Values.* Free Press, 2010.

- o **Relevance:** Argues for a science-based morality, reinforcing **Scientific Understanding (Chapter XI)** and **The Ethical Compass**.
- Ruiz, Don Miguel. *The Four Agreements: A Practical Guide to Personal Freedom.* Amber-Allen Publishing, 1997.
  - o **Relevance:** While spiritual, its emphasis on personal responsibility ("Be impeccable with your word," "Don't make assumptions") aligns with **The Architect of Self** and ethical communication.

For The Power of Story and Symbol (The Resonant Echo - Chapter VI):

- Campbell, Joseph. *The Hero with a Thousand Faces.* Princeton University Press, 1949.
  - o **Relevance:** The seminal work on the monomyth, directly supporting **Mythological Archetypes (Chapter XII)** and **The Resonant Echo**.
- Harari, Yuval Noah. *Sapiens: A Brief History of Humankind.* Harper, 2015.
  - o **Relevance:** Discusses the role of shared fictions and collective narratives in human cooperation and societal development, reinforcing **The Resonant Echo** and **The Grand Tapestry**.

II. References for Addenda

These additions would specifically bolster the secular and academic grounding of the Addenda, particularly those dealing with more esoteric or spiritual concepts.

For The Cosmic Tapestry (Addendum I) & Extraterrestrial Kinship (Addendum III):

- DeGrasse Tyson, Neil. *Cosmos: A Spacetime Odyssey.* National Geographic Books, 2014.
  - **Relevance:** Modern scientific exploration of the universe, fostering **The Cosmic Reverence (Addendum XIV)** and grounding cosmic connections in scientific reality.
- Sagan, Carl. *Cosmos.* Random House, 1980.
  - **Relevance:** A classic that beautifully blends scientific rigor with a sense of awe and wonder, reinforcing **The Cosmic Reverence** and the idea of our cosmic origins.
- Loeb, Avi. *Extraterrestrial: The First Sign of Intelligent Life Beyond Earth.* Houghton Mifflin Harcourt, 2021.
  - **Relevance:** A contemporary scientific perspective on the search for extraterrestrial intelligence, offering a grounded approach to the topic.

For The Subconscious Oracle (Addendum II):

- Freud, Sigmund. *The Interpretation of Dreams.* (Various editions, first published 1899).

- - Relevance: While foundational and debated, it's a key historical text on the subconscious and dream analysis, relevant to the idea of an "oracle."
- Jung, Carl G. *Dreams, Memories, Reflections.* Vintage Books, 1961.
  - Relevance: Jung's work on dreams and the collective unconscious provides a rich psychological framework for interpreting subconscious messages.
- Goleman, Daniel. *Emotional Intelligence: Why It Can Matter More Than IQ.* Bantam Books, 1995.
  - Relevance: Discusses the role of emotional awareness and intuition, relevant to accessing inner wisdom.

For The Five Laws of Existence (Addendum VII):

- Tolle, Eckhart. *The Power of Now: A Guide to Spiritual Enlightenment.* New World Library, 1997.
  - Relevance: While spiritual, its core emphasis on presence aligns with "Everything is Here and Now."
- Chopra, Deepak. *The Seven Spiritual Laws of Success: A Practical Guide to the Fulfillment of Your Dreams.* Amber-Allen Publishing, 1994.
  - Relevance: While spiritual, it presents universal principles (like the Law of Karma/Giving and Receiving) in a digestible format. (Use with caution, emphasizing the secular reinterpretation).

For The Sacred Flame of Being (Addendum VIII):

- Nagoski, Emily. *Come As You Are: The Surprising New Science That Will Transform Your Sex Life.* Simon & Schuster, 2015.
  - **Relevance:** Provides a science-based, compassionate approach to sexuality, emphasizing pleasure, consent, and body wisdom.
- Brown, Brené. *Daring Greatly: How the Courage to Be Vulnerable Transforms the Way We Live, Love, Parent, and Lead.* Gotham Books, 2012.
  - **Relevance:** Explores vulnerability and shame, which are often intertwined with discussions of sexuality and authenticity.

For The Great Cycle (Addendum IX):

- Kübler-Ross, Elisabeth. *On Death and Dying: What the Dying Have to Teach Us About Living.* Scribner, 1969.
  - **Relevance:** A seminal work on the stages of grief and the psychological aspects of dying.
- Chödrön, Pema. *When Things Fall Apart: Heart Advice for Difficult Times.* Shambhala Publications, 1997.
  - **Relevance:** While Buddhist, offers secular insights into embracing impermanence and navigating suffering, relevant to the acceptance of cycles.

For The River of Now (Addendum X):

- Kabat-Zinn, Jon. *Full Catastrophe Living: Using the Wisdom of Your Body and Mind to Face Stress, Pain, and Illness.* Delta, 1990.

- - Relevance: The foundational text for Mindfulness-Based Stress Reduction (MBSR), emphasizing presence and body awareness.
- Siegel, Daniel J. *Mindsight: The New Science of Personal Transformation.* Bantam Books, 2010.
  - Relevance: Explores the neuroscience of mindfulness and presence, supporting the scientific grounding of **The River of Now**.

For The Luminous Spark (Addendum XI):
- Brown, Brené. *The Gifts of Imperfection: Let Go of Who You Think You're Supposed to Be and Embrace Who You Are.* Hazelden Publishing, 2010.
  - Relevance: Discusses joy, play, and gratitude as essential for wholehearted living.
- Huizinga, Johan. *Homo Ludens: A Study of the Play-Element in Culture.* Beacon Press, 1955.
  - Relevance: A classic philosophical exploration of the importance of play in human culture.

For The Living Vessel (Addendum XII):
- Van der Kolk, Bessel A. *The Body Keeps the Score: Brain, Mind, and Body in the Healing of Trauma.* Viking, 2014.
  - Relevance: Explores the profound connection between mind and body, and how the body holds wisdom and experiences.
- Damasio, Antonio. *Descartes' Error: Emotion, Reason, and the Human Brain.* Putnam, 1994.

- o **Relevance:** Argues for the inseparable link between emotion, reason, and the body in decision-making and consciousness.

For The Weave of Repair (Addendum XIII):
- Rosenberg, Marshall B. *Nonviolent Communication: A Language of Life.* PuddleDancer Press, 2003.
    - o **Relevance:** Provides practical tools for compassionate communication and conflict resolution.
- Lederach, John Paul. *The Moral Imagination: The Art and Soul of Building Peace.* Oxford University Press, 2005.
    - o **Relevance:** Explores principles of conflict transformation and reconciliation on a larger scale.

For The Cosmic Reverence (Addendum XIV):
- Keltner, Dacher. *Awe: The New Science of Everyday Wonder and How It Can Transform Your Life.* Penguin Press, 2023.
    - o **Relevance:** A recent scientific exploration of the emotion of awe and its benefits.
- Sagan, Carl. *Pale Blue Dot: A Vision of the Human Future in Space.* Random House, 1994.
    - o **Relevance:** Continues the theme of cosmic perspective and our place in the universe, inspiring reverence.

For The Wisdom of Humility (Addendum XV):

- Popper, Karl R. *The Logic of Scientific Discovery*. Routledge, 1959.
  - **Relevance:** Explores the philosophy of science, emphasizing falsifiability and the provisional nature of scientific knowledge, which cultivates intellectual humility.
- Taleb, Nassim Nicholas. *Fooled by Randomness: The Hidden Role of Chance in Life and in the Markets*. Random House, 2001.
  - **Relevance:** Discusses the human tendency to underestimate randomness and uncertainty, reinforcing the need for humility.

For The Ethical Footprint (Addendum XVI):

- Hawken, Paul (Ed.). *Drawdown: The Most Comprehensive Plan Ever Proposed to Reverse Global Warming*. Penguin Books, 2017.
  - **Relevance:** Provides evidence-based solutions for environmental sustainability, grounding ethical action in practical science.
- Singer, Peter. *Animal Liberation*. Harper Perennial Modern Classics, 1975.
  - **Relevance:** A foundational text in animal ethics, relevant to expanding **Compassion (Chapter XI)** and **The Ethical Footprint** to all sentient beings.

For The Guiding Hand (Addendum XVII):

- Gladwell, Malcolm. *Outliers: The Story of Success.* Little, Brown and Company, 2008.
  - **Relevance:** Discusses the role of mentorship and opportunities in success, highlighting the importance of guidance.
- Brookfield, Stephen D. *The Skillful Teacher: On Technique, Trust, and Responsiveness in the Classroom.* Jossey-Bass, 2015.
  - **Relevance:** While focused on teaching, its principles of effective guidance and fostering learning are broadly applicable to mentorship.

For The Wellspring Within (Addendum XVIII):

- Van der Kolk, Bessel A. *The Body Keeps the Score: Brain, Mind, and Body in the Healing of Trauma.* Viking, 2014.
  - **Relevance:** Reinforces the importance of holistic self-care for mental and physical well-being.
- Porges, Stephen W. *The Polyvagal Theory: Neurophysiological Foundations of Emotions, Attachment, Communication, and Self-regulation.* W. W. Norton & Company, 2011.
  - **Relevance:** Provides a scientific understanding of the nervous system's role in self-regulation and well-being, relevant to practices for **The Wellspring Within**.

For The Living Chronicle (Addendum XIX):

- Bruner, Jerome. *Acts of Meaning.* Harvard University Press, 1990.

- - **Relevance:** Explores the role of narrative in human cognition and meaning-making.
- McAdams, Dan P. *The Stories We Live By: Personal Myths and the Making of the Self.* Guilford Press, 1993.
  - **Relevance:** Focuses on the psychological importance of personal narratives and how they shape identity.

Made in United States
North Haven, CT
15 September 2025

72485296R00184